D1432548

The Practice
of Psychotherapy

The Practice of Psychotherapy

A Guide for the Beginning Therapist

Richard C. U'Ren, M.D.

Associate Professor
Department of Psychiatry
Director
Adult Outpatient Psychiatry Clinic
University of Oregon Health Sciences Center
Portland, Oregon

Grune & Stratton

A Subsidiary of Harcourt Brace Jovanovich, Publishers

New York   London   Toronto   Sydney   San Francisco

Library of Congress Cataloging in Publication Data

U'ren, Richard C.
 The practice of psychotherapy.

 Includes bibliographical references and index.
 1. Psychotherapy. I. Title. [DNLM:
1. Psychotherapy. WM420 U75p]
RC480.5.U73 1980 616.89'14 80-13874
ISBN 0-8089-1242-9

© **1980 by Grune & Stratton, Inc.**
All rights reserved. No part of this publication
may be reproduced or transmitted in any form or
by any means, electronic or mechanical, including
photocopy, recording, or any information storage
and retrieval system, without permission in
writing from the publisher.

Grune & Stratton, Inc.
111 Fifth Avenue
New York, New York 10003

Distributed in the United Kingdom by
Academic Press, Inc. (London) Ltd.
24/28 Oval Road, London NW 1

Library of Congress Catalog Number 80-13874
International Standard Book Number 0-8089-1242-9

Printed in the United States of America

For George Saslow

Contents

Acknowledgments

I would like to acknowledge my gratitude to Roberta Beckman, my secretary, who was my best supportive therapist while I was writing this book; to Herant Katchadourian and Betty Hamburg who, respectively, bore with me and encouraged me while I was learning psychotherapy as a resident at Stanford; to Jim Shore, in whose department it has been a pleasure to work; and to Herbert Bowman, who read my manuscript with care and tactfully suggested the necessary changes.

Preface

The best advice I received about psychotherapy came from experienced supervisors I worked with during and after my residency. Oral tradition does not have the permanence of the printed word, however, and for a long time I wished there was a short book available to guide the beginning psychotherapist as I was so helpfully guided. It is the need for such a book that first inspired me to undertake this one. This book should be especially helpful to psychiatry residents as they start their work in the outpatient clinic, but I believe anyone interested in psychotherapy can learn something from the present work.

My own training was broad, and the approach to therapy I advocate in this book is broad also. My methods are borrowed from behavior therapy, crisis intervention work, supportive therapy, process-oriented therapy, insight-oriented therapy, and existential writings. Accordingly, this approach has applicability to patients with a rather wide variety of problems.

I hope that my book carries a spirit of pragmatism in the practice of therapy and a spirit of generosity in its approach to patients. I also hope that it serves to make therapy less forbidding and mysterious. Too often in the past, the learning of psychotherapy has been clouded for the beginner by technical jargon and a rather esoteric body of knowledge. After all, much of psychotherapy is a discussion between two people about the problems of living that one of them is having.

My introduction to the practice of psychotherapy represents only one approach out of many. I hope, in fact, that it will serve to stimulate the beginning therapist to branch out and learn more about the many therapies that crowd this vast field. I have hardly more than touched on such interesting areas as the various group therapies, depth psychology and psychodynamics,* or the newer psycholinguistic approaches to treatment.† These

---

*Malan DH: Individual Psychotherapy and the Science of Psychodynamics. London, Butterworths, 1979

†Bandler R, Grindler J: The Structure of Magic, vols. 1 and 2. Palo Alto, Science and Behavior, 1975

areas are important for therapists, however, as they strive to understand and help their patients, and an impressive body of literature already awaits the serious student of psychotherapy. The rewards of therapy for the practitioner include not only the joy that comes from seeing patients improve, but also the deep intellectual satisfaction that comes from learning about the impressive body of work, past and present, that has been carried out in this field.

Since I want this book to be shorter rather than longer, I will by no means attempt to cover all the areas of knowledge a therapist should control. I will assume, though, that the therapist has or soon will have some familiarity with classical descriptive psychiatry (the recognition of depression, schizophrenia, paranoia, dementia, etc.), psychopharmacology, human development, learning theory and behavioral techniques, psychoanalytic theory, and the experiential or existential points of view. This is now basic equipment for therapists and should be studied at some point in every training program.

Throughout this book I have tried to stay with the original responses that I have made to problems in therapy rather than to present a corrected picture of myself at work. Whenever I look over what I have said to patients, I can always see what I should have said, what I should have done. Since I have learned as much from my errors as from my successes, I have tried to show here not only the victories but also the mistakes, the fits and starts, and the uncertainties that inevitably mark therapeutic work.

The Practice
of Psychotherapy

Introduction

Psychotherapy is the practice of defining problems in the patient's personal life, treating symptoms, and, at its best, helping the patient to live in ways that better satisfy the enduring needs for affection and mastery. The form of this experience is usually a meeting, one or more times a week, that may continue for a short period or for a long time. Psychiatric symptoms are related intimately to demoralization, a state of mind characterized by anxiety, depression, uncertainty, indecisiveness, lack of self-confidence, discouragement, hopelessness, isolation, and so on.[1]

Anyone who practices psychotherapy has at least five major tasks to perform. First, a helping relationship with the patient must be established. Second, the patient's situation must be grasped intellectually and emotionally. Third, the patient must be helped to define problems in a specific, nonabstract way; to define a problem well is usually the first step in solving it. Fourth, the therapist needs to be able to evaluate the patient's assets and strengths as thoroughly as the problems. Fifth, the therapist should know how to do something about the problems a patient brings. If not, the therapist should know where to refer the patient. I elaborate on each of these tasks in the course of the book.

Every beginning therapist is confronted by a baffling array of therapeutic methods. Indeed, psychotherapists everywhere have their own opinions about what is necessary to help a person manage distress and improve relationships with others. In American psychiatry, three major schools hold sway: the dynamic, the behavioral, and the experiential. The dynamic school, inspired by Freud, emphasizes an understanding of childhood experiences in the genesis of current problems and an analysis of the patient's feelings toward the therapist, feelings which presumably stem from unresolved conflicts with parents. The behavioral school stresses the importance of resolving well-defined current problems in accordance with principles of learning. The experiential school emphasizes the importance of will, choice, and personal awareness.[2]

All practitioners, whatever their allegiance, obtain moderately good results. The weight of evidence shows that therapy produces more positive results than would occur without treatment. All types of therapy produce some benefits for some patients. A recent review of the outcome of psychotherapy with a variety of patients revealed that about 75 percent of them were helped.[3] There is little evidence, though, to show that any one form of therapy — psychoanalysis, behavior therapy, group therapy, or client-centered therapy — is superior to any of the others. They all have similar rates of success. Nor is there any evidence to show that long-term therapy is more effective than shorter therapy.[4,5]

Why is it that *all* forms of therapy achieve moderately good results? Probably because all of them share certain common features that promote an individual's well-being and combat demoralization. Each form, for example, has a rationale or myth which explains what the patient's problems are caused by and how they might be relieved. Each mode offers an intense, emotionally-charged, confiding relationship with a helping person or with a group of helping people. Therapists of all persuasions offer their patients new information about the nature and causes of their problems and ways to overcome them, thus generating hope. In every form of therapy, the expectations of help are enhanced by the therapist's personal qualities, status, and the setting in which he or she works. Therapists provide their patients with enough experience of success to restore morale and enhance feelings of confidence and mastery. Behavioral therapists, for example, do this by asking patients to work with them on a task or plan of change where it is impossible for the patient to fail. In other forms of therapy, the patient may feel successful when new insights are gained into the causes or effects of his or her behavior and attitudes.[6]

The upshot is that a variety of therapeutic approaches are helpful. There is no one best way to treat many of the problems that the patient brings to the therapist. Clinicians have made some promising beginnings in their attempts to match specific treatments to specific patients with specific problems, but they still have a long way to go. Therapists are therefore well-advised, as Jerome Frank[7] suggests, to acquaint themselves with different methods of treatment, to master those which best suit their own personal style, and to apply those which they judge most suitable for a given patient.

Whatever the form of therapy, though, a successful outcome seems to depend first of all upon a good relationship between patient and therapist. Therapists should be interested, understanding, respectful, tactful, and confident of their ability to help. Patients must bring an "expectant faith," as well as a capacity and willingness to profit from what the therapist offers.[8] It may be that this capacity is deeply rooted in the individual's relationship to parents. Psychotherapy is potentially useful when the patient has remained responsive to parental influences and is probably futile when such receptiveness has never existed or has been severely frustrated.[9]

This therapeutic relationship, or alliance, provides the therapist with leverage to help the patient in a variety of ways. Once patients feel the therapist understands, and has their well-being at heart, they are both more likely to collaborate in therapy and to be more susceptible to the influence of the therapist. Within the shelter of this relationship, the patient is able to cry, to be angry, to get things off his or her chest. The patient is able to talk with someone about problems and about troublesome patterns of interaction with other people. The patient may be able to define problems more clearly. The therapist may also be able to give the patient a different perspective on these problems, and provide reassurance, encouragement, support, advice, or new information. The patient and therapist may figure out new strategies for dealing with certain problems, and use special techniques to implement them. The therapist may also serve as an important model for the patient, both by his or her personal manner and by the way the work is conducted.

I cannot hope to discuss every situation that the clinician will face, of course. I hope to provide a few guideposts to direct the therapist in what is often an uncertain journey.

This book has two parts. In the first part, "Procedures," I discuss the conduct of psychotherapy. In the second part, "Workouts," I present five case examples that illustrate the application of these procedures.

REFERENCES

1. Frank J D: General psychotherapy: The restoration of morale, in

Freedman D X, Dyrud J E (eds): American Handbook of Psychiatry (ed 2), vol. 5. New York, Basic Books, 1975, p 118
2. Karasu T B: Psychotherapies: An overview. Am J Psych 134: 851–862, 1977
3. Smith M L, Grass G V: Meta-analysis of psychotherapy outcome studies. Am Psychol 132: 752–760, 1977
4. Luborsky L, Singer B, Luborsky L: Comparative studies of psychotherapies. Arch Gen Psychiatry 32: 995–1008, 1975
5. Sloan R B, Staples F R, Cristoll A H, et al: Psychotherapy Versus Behavior Therapy. Cambridge, Harvard University Press, 1975
6. Frank J D: Therapeutic factors in psychotherapy. Am J Psychother 25: 350–361, 1971
7. Frank J D: What is psychotherapy? in Bloch S (ed): An Introduction to the Psychotherapies. New York, Oxford University Press, 1979, p 15
8. Frank J D: The faith that heals. Johns Hopkins Med J 137: 127–131, 1975
9. Strupp H H: On the basic ingredients of psychotherapy. J Consult Clin Psychol 41: 1–8, 1973

Procedures

First Meeting

The therapist's goals in the first meeting with a patient are to establish a helping relationship, to get information, and to give information. It usually takes several meetings for the therapist and his patient to establish a proper relationship and to exchange the kinds of information they need in order to work together. I am unable to prescribe how much should be accomplished by the end of the very first interview simply because the amount of work that can be accomplished in the first meeting varies so much from case to case. It takes time to know a person well. Fortunately, a therapist does not have to understand everything about the patient in order to be of help. The therapist's aim is not total comprehension but understanding for action.

There is no doubt that the first interview is the hardest in the course of therapy. The therapist and the patient are strangers who are not used to each other. Therapists are faced with simultaneous tasks of understanding what are usually complicated problems, of paying attention to a myriad of verbal and nonverbal communications, of examining their own responses, of adjusting their own style to meet the patients' and of thinking what they might do for their patients. The patients, who are often at the low point of their lives are expected to reveal their problems and vulnerabilities to someone they do not know. At the same time, they are evaluating the therapist and wondering whether the therapist can help them or not. I wonder that the first meeting so often works out as well as it does.

Because the first interview is so demanding, for both the patient and the therapist, and because the rapport they establish early, often in the first interview, so frequently sets the tone for subsequent meetings, I have chosen to emphasize it in this chapter. The work of the first meeting may take several interviews to accomplish, however. The first meeting, as I am using the term, may therefore include more than one session.

Whatever their specific complaints, patients usually seek help from a therapist when they feel demoralized. Demoralization is a state of mind that results when people feel unable to cope with problems they or others around them expect them to handle. There are different degrees of demoralization, of course, but a person with a full-blown case has lost self-confidence and self-esteem. The person feels ashamed and guilty; feels that he or she has failed, tends to become isolated and feel alienated from others. The person is self-absorbed and preoccupied with avoiding further failure. Predominant moods are anxiety and depression.[1]

The complaints that patients bring to the therapist could be roughly organized under four headings: feelings, thoughts, actions, and somatic symptoms. Feelings are depression, anger, frustration, discouragement, unhappiness; thoughts are fears, obsessions, even worry about going crazy; actions are almost invariably some kind of difficulty in getting along with other people, perhaps a wife or husband, a child, a colleague, an employer; somatic symptoms are headache, stomach pain, and back trouble, the most common psychosomatic ailments. In some combination, such complaints will appear in every case that presents itself to the therapist.

The first contact with a patient is usually by telephone. I make my own appointments, and I like to talk with prospective patients or their relatives before the first meeting. I believe patients have a right to hear the voice of the person from whom they're seeking help. They may also have questions. I prefer, therefore, to have patients call me to set up an appointment. If I'm out, I return the call as soon as I can, usually before the end of the day.

Residents do not always feel this is practical in a busy outpatient clinic. Some prefer to give the clinic social worker their available appointment times and have the social worker set up the appointment with the patient. Others choose to call the patient themselves after they have heard about the case from the social worker.

If a colleague calls me and asks if I can see a patient, I ask for a brief description of the patient and the problems. If I think I can help, I say, "I'd be happy to see him. Would you have him call me at my office." If I'm out and have to return the patient's call, I say, "Mrs. A., this is Dr.

U'Ren. I got your message. Can I help you?" Many patients will immediately give a therapist a brief idea of what's bothering them – they feel depressed, for instance, or their marriage is in trouble. Then I may say, "I'd be happy to meet with you about that. Why don't we set up an appointment to talk?"

The therapist should spend a little time thinking about the patient before the first interview. Depression is the commonest psychiatric problem after adolescence, so I always think of it as a strong possibility whenever someone calls for an appointment. If a man in his late 20s calls, I also consider the possibility of a situational problem of a personality disorder. If a woman in her 50s telephones, I think first of an involutional depression. And if a woman calls and wants to make an appointment for her 76-year-old husband, I always suspect the presence of dementia or depression.

When the hour of the meeting arrives, I go to the waiting room and introduce myself to the patient. Once we're in my office and seated, the patient may open the conversation by saying why he or she came. If that does not occur, I'll start the meeting in one of two ways. If I know something about the patient in advance, I may say, "Mrs. S. told me you wanted to talk to somebody because you're unhappy. You have problems both at home and at work."

If a patient looks sad, I may start the session with an observation: "You look discouraged." A comment about a person's appearance or mood can be a powerful opener.

The patient now launches into his story. The therapist should never start the interview by asking the patient about age, marital status, or job. This information usually emerges in the course of a skillful interview. One should not subject a patient to computer questions when the patient needs a personal relationship. If specific information is needed, the therapist should wait till the end of the hour and ask for it.

Right from the beginning, of course, a therapist tries to create a helping relationship with the patient. This is done by being interested, concerned, unaffected, empathic, and respectful. In almost all kinds of successful therapy, patients say that they have no doubt that their therapists like and respect them, just as they like and respect their therapists. They also view their therapists as experienced and active, willing to engage in small talk at times, and not critical of them in a way that damages their self-esteem.[2]

Patients who do poorly in therapy often have hard things to say about their therapists. They report that the therapist failed to understand their feelings, used abstract language, depersonalized them, caused them to express intense anger, and behaved passively and neutrally. The patients who do poorly are often unsure about how their therapists feel about them.[2]

There is little doubt that patients need to feel at least some measure of empathy, warmth, and respect from their therapists if the treatment is to be successful. Acceptance of the other person — a willingness to let the person be, feel, or say what he or she wishes — is at the core of a helping relationship. Acceptance means understanding and appreciating the complexity and diversity of another person.[3]

One should assume that patients may be doing their best, within the circumstances of their life. This belief has helped me look upon patients with charity and tolerance. It has also saved me from blaming them.

A therapist should possess a helping attitude towards people and their problems that enables him or her not only to accept them, but to accept them with interest and hopefulness. A therapist who, on hearing about a patient's request, thinks "That sounds impossible. What could I ever do about that?" is less likely to be of help than a therapist who thinks, "Hmmm. Interesting problem. I don't have an obvious solution but it sounds fascinating and I'd like to hear more about it."

A good therapist should be hopeful. Patients are usually discouraged when they come to a therapist. In the following exchange, the therapist communicates hopefulness directly:

Patient: Do you think there's any way I can change things?

Therapist: I don't think there's any reason we shouldn't try. Several possibilities occured to me as you were talking.

A therapist should be generous toward a person who seeks help. In being generous at first, the therapist earns the right to take a stand later. Generosity shows by listening carefully and letting the patient do the talking, by making an effort to give a patient a desired appointment, and by providing extra time when necessary.

Patient: (over the telephone) I'd like to set up a time to see you, but I'd like to talk to you first — perhaps we could do that on the phone — about my son.

Therapist: Of course. Would you like to call me about eleven tomorrow?

Generosity also means that a therapist continually strives to understand the patient and avoids criticizing, blaming, or labeling pejoratively. A beginning therapist, for example, may feel irritated when a patient asks for Valium at the end of the first interview, and may label the patient "manipulative."

The patient's request may have other meanings, however. The patient may be telling the therapist that medicine has helped in the past and may be necessary now. The request may be a way of saying, "Please do something specific to help me." When the therapist is willing to admit that a troublesome request has more than one meaning, as in this example, he or she is acting generously toward the patient.

In addition to being generous, a therapist should be flexible. There is little reason to be dogmatic or authoritarian. A therapist should be able to vary the approach to suit each patient.

The patient was a 27-year-old woman who was depressed, overweight, and overdependent on her mother. The therapist recommended they work on the depression and the dependence. The patient said she'd see if she could lose some weight first.

Therapist: Okay. If that's where you'd like to start, it's worth a try. Let's set up a plan to see how it works.

Flexibility also refers to the ability of the therapist to use different techniques and to move easily from one treatment modality to another. A therapist may be required to move from individual therapy to marital therapy, perhaps even to family therapy, in the course of treatment with any one patient.

The therapist should encourage patients not to waste time regretting past mistakes and failures and, instead, to learn from them. The therapist, after listening to a patient's previous attempt at problem solving, may say, "You've at least discovered what hasn't worked. That's good information. There's no reason to go on like that if you don't want to." Failures are not dishonorable; they often provide useful information. Furthermore, there is no reason that patients can't try new ways to solve their problems.

A therapist must also be able to tolerate uncertainty. Uncertainty is the hallmark of clinical work. Decisions must always be made with less information than one would like, and there is no reason to expect that all one's efforts will meet with a satisfying conclusion. The therapist is often in the position of a teacher with students: the best effort should be made but one must remain in the dark about whether an impact has been made.

A sense of humor is always valuable. This means more than enjoying jokes and being witty (though these qualities can be important in therapy). A sense of humor gives us perspective, enables us to take some of the seriousness out of our problems, and helps us to relax with each other.

It is a mistake, of course, to force humor. What the therapist can do is to seize an opportunity to use it.

Patient: She was so involved as his secretary that when he had a heart
             attack she had one two weeks later. What do you think of
             that?
Therapist: Sounds to me like it's carrying empathy a bit far.

In the continuing attempts to bring depth and effectiveness to one's
work, a therapist should also remember that he or she is rarely the prime
mover in another person's attempt to change. The therapist is a catalyst, at
best. A therapist should remember, too, that not all problems can be
solved. Patients have no right to ask that their happiness be guaranteed as a
result of therapy, and therapists have no power to grant it. Even Freud
said that the best psychoanalysis could do was to help people resolve their
neurotic conflicts so that they could live better with normal unhappiness.

There are many therapies; there are many ways to help; there are many
places to find help. Patients may have any number of experiences in life
which change them, give them a different outlook, or relieve their suffering. Finding a new friend, meeting with unanticipated success, or moving
away from home may all bring unexpected and beneficial changes in their
wake. Fortuitous events over which the patient and the therapist have no
control may profoundly alter the course of therapy.

A therapist can help the interview along by remembering to talk less
than the patient and by not interrupting. As soon as the patient has
stopped, and without waiting too long, the therapist can say something. It
should be brief. It can be a direct question ("How long ago was that?"), a
statement with a questioning inflection on the end ("So you felt frustrated?"), or just a comment ("Sounds like you feel pretty discouraged.").

There are three kinds of questions: open-ended, close-ended, and multiple choice. It is best to start an interview with open-ended questions.
These place little constraint on the patient. The therapist may ask, for
instance, "What made you decide to call me last week?" As the interview
proceeds and it becomes obvious that more specific information is needed,
more close-ended and multiple choice questions can be asked. For instance,
"When your life was better, did you experience symptoms?" or "Would
you like to continue seeing me or would you prefer to think about it and
call me later?"

As the interview moves along, it is wise to paraphrase and summarize
what the patient tells the therapist. When this is done in a warm, nonjudgmental tone of voice, summaries and paraphrases convey acceptance and
understanding. I make it a point to summarize about three times during an
interview. I paraphrase more frequently.

To paraphrase is to state precisely and with vigor what your patient has said. The statement should be brief, natural to the therapist's own way of talking, and capable of capturing strong feelings. Metaphors, analogies, and figures of speech are particular useful.

Patient: I didn't want to go to the party, but I went anyway. I hardly talked to anyone.

Therapist: You sound like the proverbial horse that can be pulled to water but can't be forced to drink.

Paraphrases can be especially effective in communicating understanding and empathy.

Patient: He said he wouldn't come back under any circumstances. I can't stand it.

Therapist: You hate being alone, even though he's been gone for three months.

Paraphrases are also extremely useful for dealing with rhetorical questions or premature requests for advice. A therapist is not obliged to answer all of a patient's questions.

Patient: (having talked about some problems at work) What should I do?

Therapist: As you said, you're wondering whether you should threaten to quit or to ask your boss for more help.

Patient: Yeah. There's something else too.

*   *   *

Patient: I don't know what to do. What do you think?

Therapist: You're feeling pretty uncertain, aren't you?*

Summarizing statements, which are longer than paraphrases, should let the patient know the therapist understands the content of what the patient has said. The therapist can encourage the patient to make additions or corrections.

Therapist: (after 20 minutes of the interview had gone by) Let me make sure I understand, and please correct me if I don't have it right. You first noticed changes in your mood a year ago. These depressions seemed to come on out of nowhere, though you sometimes noticed that they hit you when you were driving

---

*I do not mean to imply that a therapist should never answer a question directly. There are times when a patient needs guidance. In that case, an appropriate response to the patient's question might be, "Well, let's look at the choices together."

home and had nothing planned for the evening. In September, you broke up with your boyfriend. In April, you moved to a new apartment, but you didn't think that bothered you especially. In the last two months, though, the depressions have become more intense and frequent. At first they came on every couple of weeks and lasted three to four hours, but now they're worse. You can still shake them somewhat by working hard, or by keeping busy, but it's more difficult than it was. Does that capture it?

By summarizing, the patient is being told that the therapist is trying to understand how the problem looks to the patient, and that it's possible for the therapist to be wrong and to be corrected. This promotes a sense of collaboration between patient and therapist, itself a powerful antidote to demoralization.

A therapist should pay attention to the language he or she uses with patients. One should never talk down, but pains should be taken to use language that matches the patient's level of understanding. A therapist might use the word "recondite" with a woman who has a Ph.D. but rarely with a man who completed only the seventh grade. Stilted language is an occupational hazard. When talking with a patient, the therapist should avoid using words like "parameters," "dimensions," "explore," or phrases such as "Could you share your feelings with me?" The therapist should consider the possibility that the use of cliches or professional jargon means that he or she is uncomfortable with the patient.

In order to concentrate on the interview, I allow no interruptions unless something urgent comes up. Then I tell the patient briefly, and in advance, if possible, why I must be interrupted.

I rarely take notes. As a beginner I tried to get everything down *verbatim,* always afraid I would miss something important. As time went by, I gradually cut down on notes and have finally dropped them altogether, except in the unusual case where an exact chronology of events is especially important.

In order to keep the patient's story clearly in mind, I silently review what I have been told. Ten minutes into the interview may find me thinking to myself, "Let's see, she's felt discouraged and unsettled for the last two months. She has trouble getting up in the morning and she doesn't study as much as she wants to, but her appetite is good and she enjoys lots of things. Then in November, something happened. I forget what. I'd better ask her."

Throughout these first interviews, the therapist is trying to size up the patient's problems. The first task is to define what they are and what the connection between them is, if any; the second task is to do something about them.

A therapist must appreciate the fact that every person functions along multiple dimensions that are constantly interacting with each other. The clinician usually pays most attention to the biologic, psychological, and social aspects of a patient's life, but at any time may also have to consider economic, cultural, environmental, vocational, political, or religious aspects.

A therapist must possess this wide-ranging view of human functioning if the totality of the person is to be seen, and how different aspects of the person's life interact in causing difficulty.

A 45-year-old physician consulted a therapist because of severe headaches which the neurologist had diagnosed as migraine. The physician was taking more and more medication to control them. The headaches, it turned out, invariably came on within 10 minutes of the time he stepped into his house after a long day at work. He dreaded going home at night because his children were noisy and always fighting. He was worried about money and whether he should continue his present over-busy job. Also, he complained that he had too much medical work to do even after he arrived home and that his wife never seemed enthusiastic when he came in the door.

It was apparent that, while this doctor had reactive cranial arteries whose distention caused the pain (the biologic dimension), the feelings he had (the psychological dimension) about his work (the vocational dimension), his money (the economic dimension), and his family (the social dimension) no doubt triggered the tension which expressed itself in migraine headaches.

A 31-year-old woman came to a therapist because she had periods of unprovoked sadness during the week. She consistently told herself she was inadequate. She had fantasies about suicide. She complained about tightness in the back of her neck which radiated into her head. From both her behavior in the interview and from her reports, the therapist concluded that she rarely initiated conversation or shared her feelings. These patterns caused trouble with her boyfriend. Also, she'd quit her job a couple months before, which annoyed her boyfriend, since he felt she should pay some of the rent.

While this woman came to a therapist for sadness (the psychological aspect) and a feeling of tenseness in her neck (the biologic aspect), social (trouble with her boy friend, associated with shyness and nonassertiveness), economic, and vocational factors all played their complicated parts.

As the therapist listens to the patient, he generates many questions in pursuit of the larger question: What's going on here? The information he needs about the patient in the first interviews can be put conveniently into six categories:

1. Current problems, as defined by the patient, along with precipitating events and the effects of the problems on the patient's life.
2. Genetic and social history.
3. Patterns of living and patterns of relating to other people.
4. Assets.
5. Mental and physical status.
6. Expectations.

THE CURRENT PROBLEM OR PROBLEMS

As defined and experienced by the patient, these include the person's complaints and their history.

Mark D. is a 30-year-old man who came to me on the recommendation of a friend. He complained that he starts thinking about mistakes he has made at work and can't stop his thoughts, though he believes they're silly. These episodes occur regularly, every three months, and last for one to two weeks. A day or two after the thoughts begin, he becomes depressed and discouraged. His mood plunges, he feels hopeless, unable to concentrate, dull, without energy, and seriously considers quitting his job. Nothing seems to help. These episodes, which come on spontaneously, have bothered him for the past 10 years.

Mrs. B. is a 38-year-old woman who was referred to me by Dr. L. for psychiatric evaluation. She's had a number of symptoms over the last two years, the latest being ear pain and a slight feeling of giddiness. Dr. L. wondered if there might not be a psychiatric problem worth investigating.

Her problems began two years ago with a depression. She was having trouble with her marriage, she was unhappy at work, and her teenage daughter, then 16, had just become pregnant and was planning to be married. Mrs. B. felt she had failed her daughter.

Her depression has continued. Her mood is low. She has trouble getting to sleep and sleeps fitfully throughout the night. She feels tired in the morning, fatigued as the day wears on, and better in the evening, after she takes a nap. She drinks at least ten cups of coffee a day. She has not gained or lost weight. Her appetite is poor. She has observed that her mood and sometimes the pain in her ear are worse when she feels resentful toward her husband or when she has to search for her drunken brother in bars late at night.

Precipitating events refer to occurrences in a person's life that seem to precede, trigger off, or worsen the patient's problems. Threats to self-esteem or to expectations (loss of a job or financial worries), separation or threat of separation and loss, injury or anticipation of injury (illness, fear of invalidism, medical and surgical procedures) are common precipitating events. The more stress that a person experiences, the more likely he is to fall prey to a significant medical or psychiatric problem. The death of a spouse seems to be the most stressful event for most people, followed by divorce, marital separation, a jail term, or death of a close family member.[4]

Mr. H. is a 56-year-old divorced man, a manager at a private club, who complains of trouble sleeping, a low mood which is worse in the morning and slightly better during the day, loss of appetite, a five-pound weight loss, no energy, feelings of hopelessness, occasional crying spells, and intermittent thoughts of suicide for three weeks. His problems began on the day he read in the newspaper that a good friend had committed suicide.

Not every complaint or problem for which a patient consults a therapist has a clear precipitating event, of course. Some problems seem to be life-long and have no discrete beginning.

I always want to know what problems of living the patient has experienced *since* the onset of his symptoms. Difficulty working, trouble getting along with other people, an inability to enjoy oneself, or even to cope with the tasks of everyday life are the commonest complications.

Since his depression began, Mr. S. has been unable to work: his lack of concentration, trouble with memory, and an inability to make decisions bothers him too much and impairs his efficiency. He gets no satisfaction from reading or watching television and says that he's irritable and cross with his wife and children.

Mrs. R. has suffered from a phobia of germs on and off for eight years. The phobia has recently returned. Following a two-week trip to Alaska, she was unable to cook meals, wash dishes, open cans, pick up around the house, or water her plants. It's come to the point where she and her boy friend go out for most of their meals and almost never entertain at home unless he's willing to do the work. Neither of them are happy about this. Mrs. R. is worried her boyfriend will leave if she continues this way.

With chronic problems, cause–effect relationships are often obscured and all the therapist sees are downward spirals. Anxiety attacks, for example, brought on by the pressure of his job, rendered one man unable to work as an air traffic controller. The depression which ensued when he quit made his anxiety attacks worse. This example illustrates the point, I think, that the longer particular problems last, the less able the therapist is to make clear distinctions between the primary symptoms the patient experiences and the problems in living these symptoms have caused. Symptoms cause problems which cause further symptoms, and so on.

THE INDIVIDUAL'S GENETIC AND SOCIAL HISTORY

Many common psychiatric problems show a hereditary component. This is true for mood disorders, schizophrenia, sociopathy, hysteria (Briquet's syndrome), alcoholism, anxiety, and obsessional illness.[5] Every patient should be asked about the presence of psychological or emotional problems in family members. The therapist should also ask about hereditary medical problems. Diabetes, pernicious anemia, prophyria, epilepsy, or Huntington's chorea are examples of medical problems that may show themselves through psychiatric symptoms.

As the influence of psychoanalysis has waned, and the value of other kinds of therapy has been acknowledged, there has come to be less emphasis on the importance of eliciting and extensively reconstructing a patient's past history. I believe this is all to the good, but it does not mean the history should be thrown out altogether. Taking a history is one of the best ways of getting to know someone. A historical understanding of the patient's life is also critical for understanding his or her present situation, since the meaning of present events is largely determined by past experiences.[6] This is clearly illustrated in times of personal crisis, when history is no longer chronologic: events in a patient's past take on the power and immediacy of present experience.

An understanding of a person's history also helps us to be more realistic about the patient and what we might achieve in therapy. I recently saw a 40-year-old man who came for help because he felt timid and anxious every time he talked to another person. He wanted to change because he felt lonely and depressed. I learned that he was neglected and finally abandoned by his parents when he was 3 years old. He was adopted into a socially and intellectually prominent family where he always felt out of place. He was constantly criticized by his foster father and compared unfavorably with his brother and sister. His self-esteem was, and had always been, very low. I might hope to help such a person handle some social situations more comfortably, but I did not expect this individual to be comfortable in other social encounters or that he'd ever become a happy extrovert, bursting with self-confidence. One cannot undo in a course of therapy all that has gone on before in a lifetime.

Patients sometimes want to talk about their past, and that's sufficient reason for a therapist to listen, though the patient should not be encouraged to ramble on historically session after session. A few patients, however, find it easier to talk at first with their therapist about their past life rather than about present problems, and then when they see that their therapist can be trusted and is not judging them, they may move on to talk about one of their present problems. Also, some patients gain self-confidence by emotionally reliving some of their early experiences. Knowing about the patient's past may, in addition, help the therapist appreciate how much the patient has changed over time.

An extensive review of the many ways childhood experiences influence adult life is inappropriate here, but a few comments to the beginning therapist are in order.

The way and the degree to which parents accept and control their child has a decisive effect on the child's personality. Parents who love and accept their child yet place a high value on parental supervision and control tend to produce an individual who takes the parents' values seriously. He or she tends to behave well, work hard in school, and perform better in structured rather than unstructured situations. Sometimes, however, such individuals lack the confidence to express warm feelings, to assert themselves, or to risk flights of inventiveness or imagination.

Children who are loved but not much controlled are likely to develop qualities of confidence, assertiveness, independence. They tend to initiate action and to do well on their own, as well as to be individualistic. Individuals raised in this kind of family tend to dislike doing things not motivated by spontaneous interests so that persistence through the monotonous parts of long-range tasks may be troublesome.

When children experience high control along with rejection from their parents, they often submit to them out of fear but with resentment and hostility. If this hostility is directed inward, towards themselves, it creates a sense of guilt, low self-confidence, and poor self-esteem. If directed at others, particularly other children, a quarrelsome tendency to withdraw frequently occurs. Forced to obey a person in authority, a child with this kind of background will comply with sour resignation. As the child gets older, resentment and hostility may show itself in a difficult and prolonged rebellion in adolescence.

Children rebel most frequently, however, when their parents show neither care nor control. Since reasons to comply with authority are weak and aggression is not restrained, the way is open for an early migration to peer groups and a career of delinquency. These individuals may show self-reliance and initiative in their life out of school, but inducements for sustained efforts of any kind are minimal and their performance in any kind of structured situation is poor.[7]

There is much more to personality development than parental attitudes, of course, but these findings give at least some guidance to the therapist who wishes to make accurate inferences about the effects of childhood on later development.

Michael Rutter, a British child psychiatrist, has summarized a vast amount of literature bearing on both the relationship between family problems and children's psychiatric disorders and the relationship between psychiatric disorders in childhood and psychiatric disorders in later life.[8] He found that broken homes, family hostility, and maternal rejection are associated with aggressiveness in children. Social disadvantage, parental neglect, and delinquent associates are often in the background of children who become delinquents themselves.

Family discord, such as quarreling and hostility, as well as family disruption, tends to be associated with disobedience, disruptiveness, destructiveness, and aggression.

Mental disorders in parents are significantly associated with psychiatric disorders in children, but the correlation between the form of the parental illness and the child's problem is quite weak. Parents with criminality or a personality disorder tend to have children who show hyperactivity or conduct disturbances, while children of neurotic parents tend to have emotional difficulties.* Parents who have schizophrenia are more than usually likely to have children who come down with schizophrenia as they mature.

Children brought up in institutions show a pattern of social disinhibition and indiscriminate friendliness, though the effect is less marked if the child is older rather than younger when he first enters the institution.

---

*The chief characteristic of a conduct disorder is abnormal behavior which gives rise to social disapproval, such as delinquency, lying, fighting, bullying, and destructive behavior. Emotional or neurotic disorders are exemplified by anxiety, depression, obsessions, hypochondriasis, or phobias.

Large family size is associated with conduct disorders but not emotional disturbances (anxiety, depression, etc.). The oldest child in a family is more likely to suffer from an emotional disturbance than he is to turn out delinquent. Low social status has an inconsistent link with child psychiatric disorders but is most often connected with persistent delinquency.

There is *some* relationship between neurosis in childhood and neurosis in adulthood, but this applies only to a minority of both children and adults. Most neurotic children become normal adults and most neurotic adults experienced their neurosis only in adult life. There is some evidence to show, however, that daughters, but not sons, of neurotic mothers have a significantly higher rate of neurosis than girls with nonneurotic mothers.

Nail biting, thumb sucking, and enuresis are not associated with neurosis either later in childhood or in adulthood. Nail biting, present in a third of schoolage children, has in fact almost no association with psychiatric disorders either in childhood or later. Thumb sucking is common and carries no particular significance. Betwetting in young children is usually a developmental disorder which occurs as a symptom by itself and has little to do with neurosis.

It is quite uncommon for a psychiatric disorder of any type in childhood to develop into a depressive illness in later life. Adult-type depressive illness rarely shows up in childhood.

Sociopathy or psychopathy is the one adult condition with reliable antecedents in childhood. Psychopaths are likely to show a wide range of repeated antisocial acts in childhood. Only about half of these children will become antisocial adults, but most antisocial adults will have shown antisocial behavior as children. Antisocial activity is more likely to persist also if a child's parents or grandparents have been antisocial. The prognosis for a child with repeated delinquent acts is quite poor. Furthermore, delinquents are different from other children before they become delinquent. They often have a history of doing poorly in school, are unpopular, are resentful of authority, are impulsive, and are often aggressive. In fact, children who are quite aggressive at one age often become delinquent when they get older.

Above and beyond these interesting generalizations are the patterns and early experiences unique to every individual. To make a link between early experiences and difficulties or strengths in adulthood is more of an art than a science. The therapist should apply whatever factual information is available when trying to link childhood and adulthood, but should always be tentative about the conclusions.

Too often the childhood or family history is only a cursory affair for the therapist, a section thrown into an evaluation because there is a blank space on a form for it. A statement such as "the patient's parents, now 66 and 68, are alive and well. No problems. No history of mental illness in the family," is weak and uninteresting. Information should be telling and concise.

Mr. S. has two problems dealing with his girlfriend's daughter, Sonja. He's quick and severe in his discipline, and he seems unable to encourage her. His father, an irritable and unhappy man, was exactly the same way with him. It's not hard to see whom he modeled after. As a result of this limiting experience, Mr. S.'s repertoire for dealing with Sonja is extremely limited. He does not know how to behave generously toward her. This leads to constant disputes between him and the woman he's living with.

With a 22-year-old woman who complained of anxiety, depression, and multiple phobias, the contribution of her childhood experience was equally clear:

She remembers feeling unhappy, uncertain, and insecure most of her life. Her phobia tends to be worse when she's not working and has lots of time on her hands. She's also very anxious socially and constantly worries she'll say something and be embarrassed. She's an only child. Her parents were 42 when she was born. They were overprotective, telling her constantly to watch out, to be careful. At the same time, they were often critical of her. She remembers that she just gave up at a certain point: "I couldn't stand up to them." As a result, she was a timid, shy, inhibited, fearful child. She's much the same as an adult.

Obviously, all kinds of experiences may influence a person's behavior and attitudes. A therapist can err by attributing too much to early childhood experiences. A person's experiences after childhood, extending right up into the present, always deserve the most careful appraisal.

A 32-year-old woman was hospitalized following a suicide attempt. She refused to work with the nursing staff and seemed to believe that only the doctor could help her. Several weeks after her admission, she confided that she had never seen a nursing staff really help patients before; only the doctor had been helpful in previous admissions. Only with an understanding of what had happened to her before in the hospital, was the therapist able to understand the patient's initial negative attitude toward the nursing staff.

PATTERNS OF LIVING AND PATTERNS OF
RELATING TO OTHER PEOPLE

Is the individual living in ways which satisfy apparently universal needs for love, variety, security, and activities that are commensurate with the person's energy level, interests, and intellectual ability?[9,10] The answer to this question is important, since an individual who is not living in ways that meet these needs is more likely than not to be psychologically unsettled. And though people clearly live in a wide variety of ways, they cannot live haphazardly without experiencing physical and emotional repercussions. As a very concrete example, people cannot limit themselves to three hours of sleep a night, drink several cocktails daily, and fail to eat regular meals, without suffering both physically and emotionally. It has been shown, in fact, that certain habits are associated with a long and healthy life. Men who eat breakfast regularly, don't snack, maintain their normal weight, sleep regularly, don't smoke, drink no more than two drinks a day, and exercise each day, live, on the average, 11 years longer than men who have four or less of these habits.[11]

In order to obtain information about how a person typically lives, the therapist focuses on how the patient spends time, alone and with other people. I often ask a person how a typical week day and a usual weekend day is spent. I want to know how much time is spent alone, what is done when alone, and how the patient feels about it. I also want to know about how much time is spent sleeping, reading, watching television, drinking, exercising, walking, daydreaming, and whether the patient takes medicine, drugs, or drinks coffee, tea, or alcohol.

What about the person's support groups? Does he or she spend time with family and close friends? With colleagues from the job? With people in a church or political group? I may also wish to know something about the patient's environment. Where does the patient live? What is the house or apartment like? Who else lives there? Does the patient talk to neighbors?

Equally important, how does the person relate to people who are valued? Does he or she tend to move toward others, away from others, or against others?[12] What consequences does this have? I always ask the patient for specific examples of his interaction with other people: "What did you say?" "What did she say in reply?" "Then what did you do?" Therapists must understand a person's interactions with others very concretely if they expect to help. The inability or unwillingness to obtain specific information from the patient is one of the commonest obstacles to successful therapy.

Information about how a person lives can be critical. It often sheds light on the individual's current problems.

A 36-year-old man came to a therapist because of severe depression, precipitated by a breakup with his girlfriend. He said that he had been more or less depressed for the past two years, though not as severely as now. When asked about the details of his life, he told the therapist that his ways of living probably had something to do with his breakup. He hadn't worked regularly in over two years, he often skipped meals, he stayed up late at night drinking, and usually woke up with a hangover. His girlfriend was fed up with this way of living.

A 32-year-old intern came for psychiatric help because of discouragement and anxiety. A major part of her problem was that her life was too busy. She had no time for herself and felt unable to do any of the things that usually gave her pleasure.

Medical or psychiatric symptoms are often indicators of unsatisfying patterns of living. In many cases, a patient's depression, anxiety, or medical symptom seems to be the result of a bad marriage, for example, or – in the case of the intern I mentioned above – a job which left her no time for herself. In other cases, though, the problem that has brought the patient to a therapist seemingly comes out of the blue – a manic episode, for example – and disrupts a previously well-ordered life.

In any case, the fact that symptoms and unsatisfying patterns of living or relating to other people are so closely bound up with each other has major implications for every course of therapy. The goals of therapy are to help the patient achieve relief from symptoms and live in ways which satisfy needs. Sometimes the therapist must treat the symptoms first before anything else can be done. When symptoms are under control and morale is better, the patient may then be in a stronger position to make changes in patterns of living. At other times, the therapist must work with the patient on the patterns before a symptom can be controlled. And, in many cases, the therapist and patient must work in both directions at once:

A 35-year-old woman was referred for therapy because of tension headaches which occurred when she had arguments with her husband and when she became too busy with her many activities. The therapist and the patient agreed to a course of relaxation for symptom relief and to a brief course of marital therapy.

Characteristic patterns of living and relating to other people are called "personality styles." When these patterns are judged to be deeply ingrained and inflexible enough to handicap a person in his or her adjustment to life or to cause him or her serious personal distress, they are called "personality disorders."[13] Both terms connote deep and enduring patterns of thinking, perceiving, behaving, and relating which have been present for a long time and are likely to persist.

The ways that a patient thinks, perceives, and relates permeate all aspects of therapy. The therapist must learn to appreciate the patient's personality in order to decide what approaches to use in therapy, in order to predict what problems are likely to arise in the course of therapy, and in order to set realistic goals for treatment.

For example, a therapist should avoid overfriendliness and argumentativeness with a patient who shows paranoid traits. Overfriendliness only seems to engender mistrust, and argumentativeness seems to strengthen the patient's irrational beliefs. A therapist may confidently use a cognitive, problem-solving approach to therapy with a patient who is proud of the ability to manage problems in an orderly, logical, rational way, but the same therapeutic approach would be all wrong for a patient with a hysterical cognitive style who is distractible, impressionable, and incapable of persistent intellectual concentration.[14]

A therapist should be able to predict that individuals who have unreasonably high standards and are extremely critical of themselves and other people will be critical of the therapist too. If the patient quits therapy unexpectedly, it may well be because he or she felt critical of the therapist when high standards of performance were not met. A patient with a pattern of pleasing other people will also want to please the therapist. If such a patient becomes discouraged with therapy, it may be because the patient is unable to express what he or she really wants for fear of displeasing the therapist.

An appreciation of personality helps the therapist set realistic goals with the patient. Personality traits impose limits on what can be achieved in therapy. A compulsive person may learn to control rituals for keeping the house tidy, for example, but will never be able to tolerate messiness the way an individual who has never been compulsive can.

ASSETS

This is a neglected area in psychotherapy. What I mean by assets are the physical, psychological, and social characteristics individuals possess that enable them to maintain self-esteem, obtain support from other people, cope with problems, and otherwise enhance their lives.

An appreciation of a person's assets gives the therapist a perspective on the individual. A 30-year-old woman who's demoralized, anxious, and demanding looks much different when you discover that in spite of her recent divorce she is raising two children, working full-time as a high school teacher, taking a night class, and socializing regularly with several friends. Demoralized patients can demoralize their therapists. Being aware of a person's assets can instill hope and optimism in the therapist which clearly affects his ability to help.

Patients sometimes need to be reminded of their strengths and their assets, since they tend to question and depreciate their abilities when they're discouraged.

Patient: I just don't think I can make it. I can't deal with my feelings about his leaving.

Therapist: I see it rather differently. You went through this once before and it wasn't easy. You managed well enough by getting out in the evenings, talking to friends, and staying on the job. That impressed me.

Therapists are too often psychopathologists and may concentrate too intently on their patients' shortcomings. They need to pay attention to the strengths of their patients as keenly as they do their weaknesses. Good therapists should bring out the best in their patients.

It may be that a person's assets are more predictive of improvement in therapy than symptoms, the qualities of the therapist, or the therapeutic procedure itself. Patients with good ego strength, as judged by their ability to cope with stress and to form meaningful personal relationships, have been found to do well in a wide variety of therapies.[15]

A careful appraisal of a person's assets also helps the therapist to be realistic about treatment goals. A 42-year-old man who has never held any job for long will not be candidate for a high-level managerial job now, regardless of his aspirations. Too much time and too many choices have passed. A 48-year-old woman who has never formed close relationships with other women satisfactorily is unlikely to form close relationships now.

I believe that a therapist should survey a patient's work history, interpersonal relationships, any special talents or skills, coping abilities, health — both physical and psychological — and intelligence.

Work

The ability to work regularly and satisfactorily demands a set of behaviors and attitudes easily classifiable as assets: reliability, punctuality, perseverance, an ability to get along with other people, and the skill to do the job. In order to obtain information about a person's willingness and ability to work, the following questions are useful:

What kinds of jobs have you held in the last five years?
Do you like the work?
Why or why not?
How do you do at it?
Have you ever received promotions?
Have you ever had problems at work?

Interpersonal Relationships

If our evolution tells us anything, it is that we are intensely social creatures. Other human beings have decisive and critical impact on us our whole life long. This category can include the patient's history of interpersonal relationships with parents, brothers and sisters, schoolmates, superiors, subordinates, friends, wife, etc. Sometimes it is necessary to obtain a comprehensive history of these past relationships in order to understand the genesis of a current problem. Even more important for therapy, though, is information about the patient's current social relationships. Useful questions include:

Who do you spend time with?
How much?
When?
What do you do together?
If you're in trouble, do you talk with somebody about your feelings or
    do you prefer to keep them to yourself?
Do you have close friends, people you can tell your innermost thoughts
    to?
Does anyone call you when they're in trouble?
How do you think you generally get along with people?
Have friends or family ever given you information about yourself that's
    been helpful to you?

Talents, Skills, Special Interests

I include this category because many people possess special abilities, sometimes overlooked, which give them a special sense of competence. During my residency, I treated a dyslexic boy whose self-esteem was very low. It was not until he discovered he had a flair for magic shows that his confidence picked up, and his classmates became interested in him. Questions which tap this area are:

> What do you like to do in your free time?
> Are there things you do that give you special pleasure or that you feel you have a special flair for?
> Do other people think you have special abilities in some area?
> Are there activities you'd like to pursue more if you could?
> What do you do during the week that gives you pleasure?

Coping Abilities

I always want to know how the person deals intrapsychically and interpersonally with expected stress (a transition from high school to college, the anticipated death of a relative, etc.) and unexpected stress (accidents, divorce, for example). There is no standard list of intrapsychic coping mechanisms (also called ego mechanisms of defense), but the most common ones are suppression, sublimation, humor, intellectualization, repression, displacement, reaction formation, dissociation, fantasy, projection, hypochondriasis, acting out, and distortion. Questions that get at this area include:

> What is the most stressful event you've experienced so far?
> How did you cope when . . . . The therapist can pick his own situation here. For example . . . when your baby was born . . . when your husband was away for six months . . . when your mother-in-law came to visit for a month . . . .
> What was the outcome?
> How did you deal with your sad/angry/lonely feelings?
> How do you think you managed it, looking back?
> Would you do it any differently?
> Did you notice any change in your body when all this was going on?

As I ask these questions, I am wondering what strategy the patient used to preserve his psychological equilibrium in the face of stress. I also want to know how he or she habitually copes with the ordinary events of everyday life. I have no precise way to grade the way a person copes, but following Vaillant's suggestion, I give a person high marks if I find that he or she uses mature (altruism, humor, suppression, etc.) rather than immature (projection, hypochondriasis, acting-out, etc.) or neurotic (intellectualization, displacement, reaction-formation, etc.) defenses.[17]

A man who has dealt with the breakup of his marriage by continuing to work, by consciously minimizing his discomfort, and by talking with friends about his feelings gets higher marks for coping than another man who also went through a divorce and says that he withdrew completely, made a suicide attempt, had to be hospitalized briefly, and is still furious at his wife.

Physical and Psychological Health

A person's physical health, or lack of it, is critically related to the sense of well-being. Medical illness, for instance, is not only handicapping physically but also weakens a person's morale and ability to cope with life's demands. The ancient Greeks considered good health the first of blessings; happiness was inconceivable without it. Emotional problems also undermine an individual's self-esteem and confidence. I usually ask about the patient's physical health first, then about emotional problems.

> How has your general health been? Have you ever had to go into hospital? If so, what for?
> How many times do you visit the doctor in a year?
> Have you ever consulted a therapist or a counselor before? If so, what for?
> Have you ever gone into a hospital for psychiatric reasons?

Intelligence

An appraisal of intelligence includes an estimate of I.Q. scores as well as an assessment of how and whether the individuals have used their intelligence at school, at work, and with other people. When a therapist sees a large gap between a reported high intelligence quotient and a history of trouble in school, at work, or with other people, the patient should be suspected of having a personality disorder or a major mental illness such as schizophrenia or an affective disorder. High intelligence gives no one immunity to emotional problems, but a high intelligence is often associated with high achievement, interpersonal skills, and athletic prowess.[17]

A therapist can get a rough idea of a patient's intelligence by the way the patient thinks, talks, and grasps concepts. I pay special attention to vocabularly and fund of information. I try to form an impression of how the patient has applied his or her intelligence to personal problems.

In my mind, if not on paper, I summarize what I have learned about the patient's assets:

This woman has a number of strengths. She's been employed regularly and has a good work record. Her psychological and physical health has been good. She has a circle of friends on whom she can rely and with whom she can talk. A couple who live next door and an exboyfriend are supportive of her. She's obviously bright, and she had an excellent academic record at college before she quit. In coping with two stressful events in her life — job change and the loss of a boyfriend — she used anticipation, suppression, and intellectualization as her major defenses.

*   *   *

Mrs. W. feels indecisive and discouraged right now, but she has several assets that should not be overlooked. She's worked regularly for the last two years as a supervisor on an assembly line. She has a crisp intelligence, and is very articulate. She has no close friends, unfortunately, and therefore must shoulder the burden of a depressed father, a clinging mother, and an irresponsible brother alone. She has always enjoyed good health and has no psychiatric history.

Sometimes a person has few assets, which should also be noted.

Mr. M.'s assets are not impressive. He has not worked regularly for ten years. His personal relationships, with one or two exceptions, are almost nonexistent. He's good at woodworking, though he's never tried to make a living at it. When stressful situations confront him, he withdraws. His physical health has been good, and he works out by jogging two or three times a week. He's never seen a therapist before. His intelligence is above average, but he was handicapped in school because of a pervasive sense of low self-esteem.

There is obviously a good deal of overlap between different assets. Most jobs require a person to get along with other people. A person copes better with problems if there is a friend to talk to. Special abilities may promote personal relationships. With each and every patient, the therapist should assess strengths as carefully as weaknesses.

MENTAL AND PHYSICAL STATUS

The mental status examination provides an important piece of data on which the therapist should base the diagnosis and formulation. The purpose of the mental status exam is to provide an accurate description of the patient's current functioning.[18] It has two parts. The first part is impressionistic. The therapist takes note of the patient's state of alertness, appearance, behavior, mood, and speech. Specifically, I pay attention to a person's physical appearance, state of health, expressions, clothes, and manner toward me (e.g., challenging, submissive, formal, too familiar, suspicious, angry, ingratiating, etc.). I try to articulate a description of the patient that would allow someone else to pick him or her out of a crowded room. A specific description shows that the therapist is really looking at the patient. A description that begins with, "The patient is a 35-year-old brown-haired man who looks depressed." is not interesting. A colorful description is much better: "Mrs. G. is a striking looking woman who has jet black hair that falls to her waist, high and prominent cheek bones, a thin aquiline nose, and thin tight lips."

I watch a person's posture and movements carefully. Does the patient sit easily or tensely in the chair? What does he do with his hands? When does he change posture? Does he show any nervous habits? At what points in his story does he look sad, drop his voice, or cry? When does he look brighter? At what points does he show anger or resignation? How is his mood? Does he look discouraged, depressed, or buoyant and euphoric? Is his mood within the normal range? Is it labile or even? Is it appropriate to the topic he is talking about? How does he rate his own mood?

Therapist: How would you rate your mood in the last couple of days (or right now)?

or

Therapist: I realize that this is only a rough estimate, but could you rate your own mood on a scale from 0 to 10, 0 being the lowest you've ever felt, 5 about average, and 10 being the highest?

Inferences about a person's thinking can be made from the rate, manner, and content of speech. For example, does the person speak quickly or slowly? Are the utterances long or short; immediate or delayed? Does the person speak loudly, softly, or monotonously? Is there anything unusual about his or her speech, such as stopping suddenly in the middle of a sentence or using words in strange ways? What does the patient talk about? Is the patient preoccupied with anything? Is the patient hypochondriacal, obsessed, phobic, or delusional?

The second part of the mental status examination is more objective.

The therapist may choose to ask a series of questions that show how well the patient remembers; whether orientation to time, place, and person is appropriate; how good the patient's judgment is; what the level of intelligence is; how well the patient concentrates and attends; and whether the patient can interpret simple proverbs at the right level of abstraction. Since the mental status examination is taught to all psychiatry residents early in their training, and other therapists can look it up in any textbook, there is no reason to go through it here.[18]

I assess the integrity of a person's cognitive processes in every case, but the extent to which I carry out the more formal part of the mental status examination varies from patient to patient. I can often obtain what I consider to be an adequate impression of a person's mental processes as he or she talks during the course of the interview. With other patients an in-depth examination is mandatory.

When the second part must be introduced, I try to do it as smoothly as possible. I never say, "I want to ask you some questions to test your memory." Instead, if a 53-year-old woman with depression complains about her memory and her inability to concentrate and I decide to investigate her complaint further, I might say, "Let me ask you some questions which will help me get a better idea of what your memory is like." I also try to ask questions about memory or orientation in the context of the conversation rather than introduce parts of the mental status examination as a special procedure.

Sometimes a therapist has no choice but to approach the questions directly. I might say, "Time is getting a bit short. Before we stop today, I'd like to ask you some routine questions." I then ask the person to tell me the date, the day of the week, the year, and so on.

As I listen to patients talk, I look for themes that may help explain why they have the problems they do. If a woman says she is depressed because her husband and her boss treat her poorly, she may be sub-assertive. If another patient who has a doctorate in psychology compares the therapist unfavorably with an earlier therapist, questions the therapist's credentials, and later in the interview says he or she has trouble getting along with colleagues, competitiveness might be one of the patient's problems.

When listening to a patient I also attend closely to my own thoughts and feelings. The impact another person has on me often gives me clues to the patient's problems. Manic or hypomanic patients make me feel like joking, for example. I often feel like consoling or putting my arm around a depressed person. I am aware of the distance, argumentativeness, and suspiciousness of a paranoid individual. With an attractive woman who has a hysterical cognitive style, I may be unable to summarize the session, not because I am distracted (I think) but because I have been unable to get concrete examples of what she is complaining about. I feel frustrated with obsessional people because their explaining and attention to the smallest details seem endless.

While no therapist would want to rely exclusively on his or her feelings to make a diagnosis, these feelings should not be ignored, either. If the therapist has strong feelings about a patient, he or she at least should wonder if these are not the same feelings the patient engenders in other people, too.

There is another reason for the therapist to pay attention to these feelings. At some point during the initial interview, the therapist has to decide whether or not he or she can help the patient. If a therapist does not like the individual, feels uncomfortable, feels lots of attraction, or feels gripped by hopelessness, it is wise to think the situation over and, if possible, talk to a colleague before committing oneself to a course of therapy. If the feelings are too strong in any direction, it may be wisest to refer the patient to another therapist.

Therapists should try to be aware of their own state of mind when talking with patients. Several times I've been ungenerous or short with patients because I was too tired or too busy, for example. More awareness would have helped me control my responses better.

There is evidence to show that a careful medical history (sometimes obtained with the help of a symptom checklist) is important in the evaluation of all psychiatric patients. The reason to be alert to the presence of medical illness is that a significant number of patients — 9 percent — who seek help through a psychiatric clinic have undetected medical illnesses which definitely or probably cause the psychiatric symptoms. Cardiovascular disorders (particularly hypertension and congestive heart failure), endocrine disorders (especially hypothyroidism), and infectious diseases (notably pneumonia) often cause symptoms that mimic psychiatric disorders. Pulmonary disorders, gastrointestinal diseases, blood disorders, central nervous system diseases, and malignancies also frequently cause symptoms that may be diagnosed as psychiatric. Depression and anxiety, psychosis, and organic brain disorders are the most frequent disorders diagnosed when the underlying causes are actually medical illnesses.[19]

I ask all patients about their current state of health, if they have any medical problems they are being treated for, what medicine (another frequent cause of symptoms which look psychiatric) they are taking, and what medical conditions they have been treated for in the past.

I pay careful attention to medical symptoms both at the beginning and during the course of therapy. I may carry out a physical or neurological examination myself, but if I feel the patient needs a more comprehensive examination than the one I am able to provide, I do not hesitate to refer him or her to a physician for further medical investigation.

I insist that all patients over 50 years old visit a physician for a medical history review, physical examination, and appropriate laboratory work if they have not done so in the past year. I tend to refer younger people to physicians if they complain of anxiety attacks, multiple physical symptoms, or a persistent single symptom such as headache, palpitations, or urinary frequency. Obviously a nonphysician therapist would want to consider referring the patient for a medical examination early on if the patient complained of medical symptoms.

I often request laboratory work for the patient for screening and diagnostic purposes. I have not routinely used a symptom checklist with my patients, but the benefits of doing so for the purpose of medical screening seem indisputable.

EXPECTATIONS

You want to know what the patient expects from you and from therapy. The gap between what a patient wants from therapy and what the therapist can provide should not be too large. I have erred several times in the first interviews by not asking the patient about his or her expectations. In one instance, I mentally constructed a neat problem list for a woman which went as follows:

1. Underassertiveness, leading to a feeling of being overwhelmed by her brother and her mother
2. Anxiety about a terminally-ill relative
3. Mild depression

I then launched into a brief summary, impressed with my own perceptiveness, about what she could do to improve her life. She merely looked at me and said, "I just want some Dalmane so I can sleep. If I can't sleep, I can't work." I should have asked about her expectations before I launched into my exposition of what I could do for her.

The therapist should ask the patient about his or her expectations of therapy carefully with no hint of a "what do you want from *me*?" tone of voice. I often ask "What would you like to get out of therapy?" "What would you like to gain for yourself from our meetings?" "Most people have certain hopes and expectations when they come to a therapist for the first time. What were yours as you were coming up here today?" This is my favorite question.

There are several items that the therapist should cover with the patient before the end of the first interview. The therapist should summarize what he or she understands about the patient's problems, come to a decision about working with the patient, tell the patient what information the therapist needs to understand the problems more completely, give the patient an idea about how the therapist works, what a course of therapy is likely to entail, and talk about phone calls, tape recordings, and fees. I try to save the last 10 or 15 minutes of the first interview for this discussion.

I believe therapists have an obligation to share their impressions with the patient, who usually wants to know what the therapist thinks about him or her. Patients also want to know if they have been understood. I go about it this way:

We have about ten minutes left in our meeting today, but the time is getting short and there are several things I'd like to mention before we stop. Here's what I understand about your situation: You're lonely and don't have the kind of steady relationship you'd like with a man. You don't have a job and don't want to work again in a department store, but you hate being on unemployment. You find yourself unable to enjoy much. Perhaps worst of all, you feel discouraged and stuck, and you don't know what to do to get yourself out of this rut.

I try to make the summary brief and succinct. I always give the patient an opportunity to make additions or corrections. The therapist and the patient must decide whether they can work together. I accept most patients who come to me for therapy, and I often say, "I think I can help you with some of the problems you've told me about."

The patients I do not accept for treatment after the initial session(s) are those who want some form of therapy other than the ones I offer. I learn about this when I ask the patient about his or her expectations. If an individual wants psychoanalysis or hypnosis, for example, I offer the name of a good analyst or a good hypnotist.

Therapist. I don't do that kind of therapy myself, but I'd be happy to recommend the names of some therapists who can.

I may also decline to treat individuals who want a form of therapy which I can do but for which I have no great taste. Hypnosis and sexual therapy are my own personal examples. I am happy to do these forms of therapy a few times a year, but a very steady diet of either would bore me.

I may also be hesitant about accepting patients who will place an in-ordinate load on me. I can manage one or two borderline or chronically suicidal patients in my practice at one time, for example, but more than that I cannot do. I break the news tactfully:

Therapist: From what you've told me about yourself and your past, you need someone, I think, who will be more available to you than I could be right now. I have the names of several good therapists that I can give you.

There are some patients who simply do not react well with me. In most cases, this occurs when they have been in therapy with someone else for a long time and find that my style is too different from what they are used to. Sometimes there is simply a personality clash. Patients will often let the therapist know about their feelings, usually by a "let me call you after I think about it" answer to the question of whether they want to go on with therapy. If the therapist senses an incompatibility, however, he or she should ask about it:

Therapist: How have you felt about talking to me during this hour?
  Patient: I don't think you understand me.

The therapist may wish to ask how and why the patient felt misunderstood. But, in my experience, a patient who says this at the end of the first meeting never comes back. I recommend helping the patient find somebody he or she can work with. I also offer to stick by patients while they look for another therapist:

Therapist: It may take a few days to find someone else. I'd be happy to stick with you until you do. If you have any other questions or need anything else, call me if you want. And if none of these people work out, get in touch and I can give you some more names.

Sometimes the first interview will come to an end and the therapist does not yet know if it will be possible to work with the patient since first interviews occasionally do not go well. It's always nice if the therapist and patient hit it off at the first meeting, but it's not the end of the world if they do not. It is unwise to reject patients too quickly; they often change dramatically between the first and second interviews.

The therapist who is uncertain about working with a particular patient can say:

Therapist: I need to know more about you before I can make any specific recommendations. I suggest we meet a few times to see if we can work together and bring some of your problems into sharper focus.

The therapist should tell the patient what further information is needed to develop a treatment program. To a woman who was depressed because she felt her husband was dominating her, the therapist might say:

Therapist: You feel your husband is making all the important decisions and you feel left out. You said you don't think there's a way out. I don't see your situation as bleakly as that. There are certain things we could practice together in here which you could use with him so that your claims are better heard. But since he's involved, perhaps the first step is to invite him to meet with us. It would certainly help me understand your situation better. Would he go for that?

To a man who complains of urinary frequency — and has no detectable urinary problem, according to the urologist — the therapist might say:

Therapist: You've mentioned three problems: an urge to go to the bathroom every hour, feelings of depression, and discomfort around other people. You've said that frequency is the problem you'd like to work on first. I have some ideas about how we might do that, but first I need more information. I'd like to know how often you urinate each day. Could you keep a daily record for me between now and the next time we meet?

Therapists should give patients an idea of what therapy is about.

Therapist: I think it would be a good idea to meet once a week. Our sessions will last between 45 and 50 minutes, though if we get our work done earlier, there's no reason we can't stop sooner. At some point in our fourth session, I'd like to spend some time talking about where we've been and where we're going. If you're getting something out of these meetings, you'll know it. If you have to ask me if you're getting anything, it probably means you aren't. At the fourth session we can decide to continue the way we are or we can decide to increase or decrease the number of meetings each week.

Some therapists can give the patient an idea of how long the therapy for certain conditions will last. They may say that a particular problem requires six months' work. I have never been able to be that precise. As far as I know, the science of psychotherapy has not advanced far enough to enable therapists to make such predictions accurately. What I do know is that the length of therapy depends to a large extent on the patient's problem and the goals of therapy.

Individuals in the midst of a personal crisis who want symptom relief may require only a few visits. Patients with personality disorders who need to change long-standing perceptual and behavioral patterns need regular attention over a long period of time. People with major mental illnesses — schizophrenia, affective disorders, paranoid conditions — require pharmacologic and supportive treatment that lasts months to years. Patients with neurotic disorders — anxiety neurosis, phobic neurosis, obsessive neurosis — may require intermittent therapy over long periods of time since these conditions often wax and wane spontaneously.[5]

Nevertheless, I have always been impressed by the variable and unpredictable outcomes that patients show in the course of therapy. Some individuals have long-standing problems that are solved or at least ameliorated after several sessions, while others have problems, seemingly easy to work on, that turn out to be intractable. It is difficult to predict the outcome of therapy on the basis of the first interview.

Three other topics — telephone calls, tape recordings, and fees — can be handled in short order at the end of the first interview.

Therapist: There'll be times when you may wish to call me. If there's something you don't understand about collecting information between sessions, please do so. Also, if something comes up that you don't feel can wait till the next session, you can call. My phone number is in the white pages of the telephone book, or you can get me through the operator here. I'm happy to receive calls but I like to keep them short, two to five minutes.* If a problem comes up between sessions that needs more than a short discussion, I'll be happy to set up an extra appointment for you. Occasionally, too, I like to use a tape recorder during the session. I'll always ask your permission first and if you find that it's bothersome, we can turn it off. I need to listen to myself sometimes and at other times it saves from me taking notes.

---

*If a therapist has a large practice, he may be forced to be less available to his patients. As a colleague in private practice said, "Carrying 30 to 40 patients a week makes it necessary for me (and most therapists I know) to be inaccessible to frequent demands. Otherwise it seems you're on duty 24 hours a day. An answering service provides a neutral (usually) buffer which allows (1) accumulation of calls if you're away; (2) some discretion about which calls to return."[20]

An important principle to keep in mind is that ways of interacting ("norms") between people are formed early in their relationship and are hard to change later. Wise therapists will set the norms for tape recorders and phone calls early. If you want to make a tape recording but fail to mention it until the tenth therapy session, it is very hard to bring up.

Fees for psychotherapy are based on a sliding scale of charges in the clinic in which I work; the patient pays what he or she can afford on the basis of gross income and the number of people in the family. Many patients also carry insurance that covers a proportion of the cost.

Patients who apply for care are asked about their financial status by interviewers at the outpatient clinic and assigned a number which designates what percent of the charge they'll be held responsible for paying — 100 percent, 75 percent, 50 percent, etc.

The fees charged for psychotherapy in the clinic are very reasonable, but I urge residents to discuss the fee explicitly with any patient who is responsible for more than 50 percent of the bill and has no insurance. The resident will ask the patient if he or she knows what the charges are. They explain how the fee was determined (if the patient did not understand it before) and may refer the patient back for another financial screening if they feel the fee has been set too high for the patient.

For private patients, I state that I charge 60 dollars an hour, and I wait for the response. Most people expect to pay a fee and know approximately what psychotherapy costs. If the patient nods, I say, "I bill at the end of each month," and the issue is usually settled. If a patient shows surprise, I ask him if he can afford the fee. If not, there are other questions to ask. The first is, "Do you have any insurance?" Another is, "What could you afford to pay, by the week or by the month, for psychiatric care?" If he or she does not know, I might say, "Well, why don't you think about it over the next week and we'll talk about it at our next meeting."

Sometimes, though in a minority of cases, I'm willing to agree to a payment plan.

Therapist: I realize that 240 dollars a month is a substantial amount. Some people prefer to pay 50 dollars a month while they're in treatment and continue paying later. That's all right with me as long as we come to an agreement about it.

If reducing fees seems to be the thing to do, the therapist has to decide how far to go. The patient may try to set the limit at 30 dollars, for example. I might say, "I'm willing to lower the fee to 40, but I'm afraid that's as low as I can go." I always make it a point to ask the patient if there are any questions before I end the interview, and after the next appointment is made, we stop.

Now the door is closed and you're alone in your office. A therapist ought to allow 10 or 15 minutes between appointments so that thoughts can be gathered, a note dictated, and preparation made for the next patient. If there's not enough time to write or dictate, at least make some notes so it can be done later. I believe the psychiatric evaluation should usually be written after the first visit. If this is put off until the third or fourth visit, there is usually too much information to organize. Of course there will be gaps in the information the therapist needs after the first interview, but these gaps can be noted at the end of the report and filled in at later meetings.

The report should not be too long. Anything much over three typewritten pages is too much for a busy person to read. The Appendix contains an example of a typical report. There are some points I would like to expand on, however.

The first part of the report should include a flowing narrative account of the patient's problems: What is bothering the patient, what brought it on, and what have the consequences been?

Mrs. H. is a 22-year-old woman who's been picking her face and her fingernails since she was 4 years old. She doesn't remember any precipitating event. She wants to stop picking because of recurrent infections on her face. She also picks her cuticles, fingernails, and any other blemish on her body. She picks most when she's at home alone with nothing to do. She's tried behavior therapy and hypnosis but nothing has worked.

In this writeup, I went on to say a few things about her past history, her current way of living, her assets, and how she behaved toward me in the interview. The report, in this case, was brief. Beginning therapists need the help of an outline, but in any case they should strive for concision in their reports. I have seen perfectly adequate workups which contained only the history of the present problem, an informal mental status examination, a problem list, and a tentative treatment plan. Further significant information can be included in progress notes.

In your workups, avoid tired phrases. "The patient states . . ." should be avoided or at least used sparingly. "He said . . ." or "She told me . . ." helps break up the monotony. Don't hesitate to use paragraphs. A solid sheet of sentences, written or typed, will fatigue the most interested reader.

Toward the end of the report, I write down a list of what I think are the patient's problems. One 30-year-old woman's list ran as follows:

1. Persistent neck pain following a car accident 6 months ago.
2. Marital problems (husband often absent, unaffectionate, unhelpful around the house, drinks every night).
3. Trouble handling the children (daughter too active, son has frequent tantrums).
4. Feelings of isolation and no one to talk to (no job at present, few friends, loss of social network upon leaving Seattle).
5. Depression/discouragement with all of the above.

A 40-year-old man's list went as follows:

1. Depression and anxiety over impending marital breakup.
2. Social anxiety in a large number of situations associated with lack of assertiveness and social isolation.

Problems can be added or subtracted from the list in subsequent sessions. There is no reason to think that one's first problem list is infallible. But what it does is to provide the patient and the therapist with a focus at the beginning of treatment.

I always try to formulate what I understand about my patient. To formulate is to express, in precise form, the individual's problems and strengths. My formulation of the problems and assets of the 30-year-old woman with neck pain following her car accident was as follows:

This woman is demoralized by all the problems in her life: her neck pain, her marital problems, her difficulties handling the children, and her physical isolation. She was having trouble with her husband before her mishap 6 months ago, but the accident and the pain she's felt since has increased her discouragement and further diminished her morale. Her chronic pain lowers her stamina and her family problems diminish her ability to deal more effectively with her pain. She's unable to relax, for example, because of her preoccupations and her troubles. She has difficulty getting out and doing things that bring her pleasure and satisfaction — talking to friends, going swimming, finding a new job, etc. She's lacking confidence. To me, her isolation and lack of support from others, especially from her husband, are the most striking facts of her distress. I suspect her pain is one way of obtaining care, concern, support, and interest from others she so desperately needs.

On the other hand, she has several assets. Her work record is good. She grew up in a stable family. Unfortunately, her network of friends has been disrupted when she and her husband moved from Portland so she has no one to talk to. She has coped well with stress in the past by talking with others and by keeping busy. Her physical and mental health has been good, her intelligence above average.

The therapist cannot say everything that comes to mind when formulating. The interactions between physical symptoms, psychological states, and interpersonal relationships are always complicated and may tempt one to engage in endless speculation. Say briefly what is important and have done with it. It can always be revised if further information comes in.

The psychiatric formulation of each and every person's case will have its own emphasis. When a person is in crisis, the precipitating stress, the psychological symptoms, and the consequences of the symptoms in the person's life should be highlighted in the formulation. The contribution of the patient's patterns of living and past history to the current problem can be articulated at some other time. Many problems have no precipitating event, such as the case of the 22-year-old woman who had picked her face and fingernails for 18 years:

This woman has a habit disturbance that has been present for a long time. She recalls no precipitating event. Recurrent infections on her face, and some self-consciousness about the condition of her skin are what bother her. She comes from a stable, close family and lives a reasonably satisfying and regular life. She has a wealth of assets, though according to her, her circle of friends could be larger.

When I cannot formulate a case after the first meeting, I leave the formulation out of the report and do it when I have more information.

Following the formulation, I try to make a formal psychiatric diagnosis. If I do not have the relevant information, I defer the diagnosis. I have begun to use the multiaxial classification system proposed in the latest edition of the diagnostic and statistical manual of the American Psychiatric Association.[13] There are five axes in this system, and it is recommended that every patient receive an evaluation on each axis. The five axes are: clinical psychiatric syndromes, personality disorders, physical disorders, severity of psychosocial stresses, and the level of adaptive functioning in the past year. As the last item of business in the psychiatric report, I write out a plan of approach to the patient's problems.

After the first interview with a 28-year-old woman who had a long history of lying, who was unable or unwilling to tell anyone her thoughts and feelings, who tolerated criticism very poorly, and who particularly had trouble getting along with other women, my plan of approach read:

1. I need more information about

    a. Why she moved back to Portland 6 months ago. I suspect she had trouble with her friends in San Francisco, and the description of those difficulties illustrate some typical self-defeating patterns of thinking and acting. If I knew what those problems were, I'd have a better idea of her self-defeating patterns of thinking and behaving.

    b. Her assets.

    c. What her family is like.

2. I have asked her to keep a written daily record of the times she lies during the week as well as the circumstances under which she does so.

3. My thoughts about treatment are tentative. I suspect that she lies when she feels inferior or criticized. She may be able to learn other ways of behaving when she feels those ways.

After seeing a 35-year-old woman whose depression was associated with a recent unhappy move to Oregon, the absence of any close friends, and her husband's habit of making all the important decisions for the family, my plan was:

1. I need more information about her.

    a. How she spends a typical day.

    b. How she eats, sleeps; whether she drinks, etc.

    c. What her upbringing was like.

    d. What she does, or can do, that brings her pleasure and satisfaction.

2. I have not decided whether I should undertake therapy with her alone or invite her husband in for marital therapy. We can decide that together in the near future.

3. We have agreed to meet two or three times in order to see if we can understand her problems better. I'll see her next week.

Writing or dictating the psychiatric report is always hard, even for experienced therapists, but it's important and necessary. To put information and ideas on paper requires discipline, organization, and thought. And clear thinking, after all, is imperative for proper diagnosis and treatment.

REFERENCES

1. Frank JD: General psychotherapy: The restoration of morale, in Freedman DX, Dyrud JE (eds): American Handbook of Psychiatry (ed 2), vol. 5. New York, Basic Books, 1975, p 118

2. Strupp HH, Fox RE, Lessler K: Patients View Their Psychotherapy. Baltimore, The Johns Hopkins Press, 1969, p 80

3. Gilmore S: The Counselor-In-Training. Englewood Cliffs, N.J.: Prentice-Hall, 1973, p 147

4. Holmes TH, Rahe RH: The social readjustment rating scale. J Psychosom Res 11: 213–218, 1967

5. Goodwin DW, Guze SB: Psychiatric Diagnosis (ed 2). New York, Oxford University Press, 1979

6. Frank JD: What is Psychotherapy? in Bloch S (ed): An Introduction to the Psychotherapies. New York, Oxford University Press, 1979, p 19

7. Becker WC: Consequences of different kinds of parental discipline, in Hoffman ML, Hoffman LW (eds): Review of Child Development Research, vol. 1. New York, Russell Sage Foundation, 1964, pp 189–199

8. Rutter ML: Relationships between child and adult psychiatric disorders. Acta Psychiat Scand 48: 3–21, 1972

9. Linton R: The Cultural Background of Personality. New York, Appleton, 1945

10. Saslow G: On the concept of comprehensive medicine. Bull Menninger Clin 16: 57–65, 1952

11. Belloc NB, Breslow L: Relationship of physical health status and health practices. Prev Med 1: 409–421, 1972

12. Horney K: Our Inner Conflicts. New York, Norton, 1945, pp 48–96

13. DSM-III Draft: Diagnositc and Statistical Manual of Mental Disorders (ed. 3). Washington, D.C., American Psychiatric Association, 1978, p K: 1

14. Shapiro D: Neurotic Styles. New York, Basic Books, 1965, pp 103–133

15. Frank JD: General psychotherapy: The restoration of morale, in Freedman DX, Dyrud JE (eds): American Handbook of Psychiatry (ed 2), vol. 5. New York, Basic Books, 1975, pp 117–132

16. Vaillant G: Theoretical hierarchy of adaptive ego mechanisms. Arch Gen Psychiatry 24: 107–118, 1971

17. Sears, RR: Sources of Life Satisfaction in Gifted Men. Am Psychol. 32: 119–128, 1977

18. Melges FT: Mental status examination, in Rosenbaum CP, Beebe JE (eds): Psychiatric Treatment. New York, McGraw-Hill, 1975, p 529

19. Hall RCW, Popkin MK, Devaul RA, et al: Psychiatric illness presenting as psychiatric disease. Arch Gen Psychiatry 35: 1315–1320, 1978

20. Van Rheenen FJ: Personal communication, 1979

Defining Problems

Some people may feel so overwhelmed, so demoralized, by their problems that they are not even able to define them. Others have never learned to define their problems clearly. To define problems with a patient gives a focus to therapy, and also serves to raise morale. If the patient can define the problems, he or she has a better chance of coming to grips with them.

Therapists, if they listen carefully enough, can often discern what is bothering their patients. The patients usually start by describing their mood or feelings, their thoughts, their behavior (or someone else's), or their physical symptoms. I always put their initial complaints first on the list of problems I silently construct during the interview.

But what's behind these complaints? No sustained feeling exists as a thing in itself, independent of what one does. Suffering is intimately connected with the ways one lives and relates to other people It exists only in a context.

This context has biologic (medical), characterologic, interpersonal, and situational dimensions that are always important to understand, and in some cases economic, social, and cultural considerations should be included. A therapist learns in time how much weight to assign to any one of these factors as it contributes to the patient's problems.

For example, the commonest psychiatric complaint, depression, is often associated with personal or interpersonal difficulties or loss, but the therapist must always be alert to other causes of depression. Schizophrenia, especially in young people, may disguise itself as a depression. Many kinds of medical illness present themselves as depression, as do many forms of brain disease. Some patients have depressive temperaments. A chaotic pattern of living or too many changes in one's life within a short period of time may contribute to a depression, as can lack of money, loss of religious belief, or political misfortune.

Sometimes a therapist can construct a comprehensive list of problems with the patient within a session or two. At other times patients hold things back, like the young woman who complained of intermittent depression for a year but neglected to tell the therapist that she was having a turbulent affair with a married man during the same period. But even patients with secrets will reveal what is really bothering them once they trust the therapist, though this may take a while. Other patients genuinely do not know what their underlying problems are. (They may be unconsciously denying them, but the therapist cannot differentiate between denial and not knowing.) Underlying problems may in fact be so hidden that they are first announced only by physical signals. A woman developed trouble swallowing two months before her husband told her he was having an affair with another woman, for instance. Another woman had crying spells for six months — she could not explain them, she just felt sad — before she discovered her husband was planning a divorce. When a symptom appears disassociated from a context, in fact, the therapist should be suspicious, remain patient, and continue to seek for information.

To sum up, patients complain about changes of mood, feeling, behavior, or bodily functioning. These complaints occur in the context of interpersonal problems, unhappiness about work, lack of money, physical illness, and so on. The problem list you construct with a patient should include the complaints and the context, whenever possible. Thus, a 38-year-old woman's list was:

1. Depression and loneliness.
2. Impending divorce.
3. Not enough money to live on.
4. Lack of a job.
5. Concern about what to do with the children if she goes to work.

Depression and loneliness were the leading complaints brought to the therapist. The other problems made up the context of those symptoms.

A 57-year-old man's list was:

1. Persistent feelings of depression and anxiousness.

2. Irritability and temper tantrums with family members.
3. Insecurity about present job.
4. Concerns about health.

The first two problems were the ones mentioned by the man and his wife. The third and fourth problems defined the context.

People differ in their ability to define their problems, of course; so do therapists. If I were asked to identify the most common problem that beginning therapists have, I would say that it is the failure to obtain specific information from patients. How often have I seen therapists struggling with highly inferential concepts like "dependence" or spending inordinate amounts of time gathering historical information when attention to a patient's present problems, revealed by specific examples, provides such rich opportunity for successful therapeutic intervention. For instance, a 32-year-old woman comes for therapy and says she's depressed. You ask her why and she says, "My marriage." You want to know specifically what it is about her marriage that's bothering her. You need details, specific information.

Therapist: What about it gets you down?

Patient: I don't feel like he includes me in decisions any more.

Therapist: Any recent examples?

Patient: On Saturday morning he decided we'd go camping overnight. He didn't even ask me about it, he just decided.

If a patient can define problems this specifically with a therapist's help, therapy is off to a good start. In this case, the husband was invited to come in for the next session and the therapist worked on ways the couple could share decision making.

Other patients will have a harder time. If an intelligent person has trouble getting along with other people and does not know why, the therapist can assume the problem is a difficult one. If the patient had the needed information, he probably would have done something about it long ago.

A patient may unknowingly have a pattern of behavior that puts people off, for example. In such a case, both the therapist and the patient need specific information about what the patient does. The therapist can obtain this information by making his or her own observations about the patient during the interview, by observing the patient in a therapy group, and by asking the patient to get information from other people. Information from friends, acquaintances, or relatives is often invaluable.

A 30-year-old man came to a therapist because he was depressed and lonely. He had no friends. Neither he nor the therapist could understand why. After some encouragement and role playing in therapy, the patient asked an acquaintance how he, the patient, came across with other people. The acquaintance told him he was too critical. The patient had never known that before. That was indeed the information that allowed therapy to proceed.

If relatives or acquaintances are unavailable as a source of information — and they often are not, since patients often do not want other people to know they are seeing a therapist — there is another important way of obtaining information: by making inferences from the specific examples the patient brings the therapist.

A 42-year-old man complained that he couldn't maintain a relationship with a woman beyond three months. He didn't know why.

Therapist: Have you and your girl friend had any problems in the last week?

Patient: Yes. She got mad at me.

Therapist: What happened?

Patient: I thought we might go out together Wednesday. I called her. She said she'd like to but she'd better stay home with the kids since she'd been out so much lately.

Therapist: So what did you do?

Patient: I said, No problem. I'll go downtown and have a drink with some friends.

Therapist: What did she do?

Patient: She got angry.

From an example like this, a therapist is able to generate a lot of ideas about why this man has trouble with women. He might wonder about the man's ability to empathize with his girl friend, to see her point of view. He might wonder if the man is the sort of individual who punishes other people when he does not get his way. He might wonder if the man is unable to support his friend when she's tied down. He might wonder about the man's ability to come up with compromise solutions that would allow the two of them to get together.

These are ideas. The therapist does not know yet whether they are good ideas or not, but he or she keeps them in mind and may be able to confirm them as more information becomes available. I do not hesitate to add my own observations to a person's list of problems, though I may not wish to share them with the patient until a later date.

I believe that many of the behavioral patterns that cause individuals to experience interpersonal problems can be found in the following table. In many cases, the therapist will be able to identify the troublesome patterns during the interviews with the patient (Table 1).

TABLE 1
Troublesome Behavioral Patterns

I. Problems of Communication
  A. Verbal Problems
    1. Unvarying content: too many anecdotes or trivial details, speech too abstract or formal, themes of hypochondriasis or paranoia
    2. Quantity: too much or too little
    3. Tempo, tone, and volume of voice
    4. All-or-none patterns of thinking (expressed in behavior and speech)
  B. Nonverbal Problems
    1. Posture
    2. Lack of eye contact
    3. Dress

II. Behavioral Problems
  A. Too little support or reinforcement/criticalness
  B. Too much or too little initiation of ideas or activities
  C. Lack of sharing, inability to share decision-making
  D. Too little or too much assertiveness or control
  E. Defensiveness, sensitivity to criticism

III. Problems of Emotion or Mood
  A. Erratic or cyclical moods, e.g., cyclothymia, manic-depressive illness, premenstrual mood changes
  B. Anger outbursts
  C. Bland mood

IV. Troublesome Habits or Idiosyncracies (drinking, drug abuse, lying, irresponsible behavior, etc.)

This table is meant to be provisional and heuristic, not exhaustive. Most of the behavior a therapist observes in the interview with the patient falls into category I. From specific examples presented by the patient, the therapist either makes inferences or obtains direct information about the patient's troublesome behavior that fall into categories II, III, and IV as well as I.

From talking to a woman about her marriage, for example, the therapist learns that her husband often criticizes her, gives her little support, does not include her when he makes decisions, and gets angry when she asks him to share the housework. While interviewing a man who has a long-standing history of trouble getting close to people, the therapist observes that he talks at a highly abstract level, goes on too long, and looks at the therapist infrequently. In both cases, the therapist should note the troublesome patterns and consider them seriously as candidates for the focus of therapy.

A therapist should always ask for specific examples when a patient uses abstract language. Patients will say, for example, that they are too *dependent,* that they feel a lot of *hostility,* that they cannot control their *impulses,* that they have *communication problems,* or that they are *inadequate.* Therapists should not let patients use those words unless they are willing to attach specific meanings to them. A therapist can say, for instance, "You've said several times you're too dependent on your boyfriend. What do you mean? Can you give me some specific examples of times you've considered yourself too dependent?" Or, "How do you act when you're 'hostile'? How would I know it? Do any specific examples come to mind?" Specific examples are the great clarifiers.

Once the therapist has a specific understanding of the patient's problems, he or she goes to work. A problem list of a 40-year-old man looked like this:

1. Mild depression with sleeplessness, lack of energy, and sadness.
2. Marital problems (husband complains wife is away too much and seems to be losing interest in the marriage).
3. Dissatisfaction with work.

The first thing I did with this man was to ask what problem he wanted to start with. He said that his marital problems were bothering him the most. We started work there.

Sometimes it may be hard to know what problem to start with in therapy. In order to decide this with a patient, I pay attention to the amount of time a patient spends talking about a particular problem. This gives me an idea of what's bothering the patient the most. I also judge the urgency of the problem. Any life-threatening problem automatically gets top priority in treatment, for example. I also pay attention to the amount of impairment a particular problem has caused the patient.

A 48-year-old woman consulted a therapist because of two problems.

The first was her job. She didn't get along with her supervisor. Whenever this came to a crisis, she developed diarrhea which sometimes lasted as long as a month. The second problem was her husband, an invalid, for whom she had to be on call constantly. The diarrhea greatly impaired her ability to work. Her problems with her supervisor assumed priority over problems with her husband since they were more threatening to her immediate livelihood.

In determining what problem to approach first, therapists also have to consider which problems they know how to treat and which problems they do not. This is not always just a matter of skill and knowledge, either. Some problems simply cannot be defined as clearly as others. I believe therapists should try to work on familiar ground where they feel competent. For me, the more specific the problem, the more likely I am to approach it first in treatment.

The therapist of course has a say about what problems will be worked on. For example, the list of problems of a 36-year-old woman read:

1. Manic-depressive illness, under control.
2. Nonassertiveness in many social situations.
3. Inability to express feelings adequately with people.
4. Lack of trust.

Looking at that list, I would probably choose to start work on either number 2 or number 3 rather than problem number 4, but I would want to know what the patient has to say about lack of trust. A discussion about trust could lead in a promising direction. I would ask her, for example, what she means by "lack of trust." Who's involved when she feels that way? If she says that it's her husband, I might ask what he does or says to make her mistrustful, whether anything has happened in the past between them to cause lack of trust, and so on. The therapist might learn that her husband's angry threats and past infidelity evoke her lack of trust. The appropriate treatment then might be marital therapy.

But if a problem (such as lack of trust) cannot be defined so precisely, even after a discussion, the therapist should probably leave it alone for the moment. Suppose, for example, that the woman above, when asked what she wanted to work on first, had said lack of trust, though a discussion she and the therapist had previously had was not productive.

Therapist: What's number 2 on your list?

Patient: My agreeableness.

Therapist: And by that you mean that you agree with people when you

>don't feel like it and you feel annoyed with yourself after-
>wards?
>
>*Patient:*   Yes.
>
>*Therapist:*   Do any specific examples come to mind?

In other words, the therapist has chosen to pass by one problem in favor of another. Sometimes, too, it is best to let a particular problem be. Some problems are insoluble. Other problems that are inaccessible at one time become approachable at another as the patient changes, as the situation alters, or as new information becomes available.

The therapist and the patient may have to revise the patient's list of problems as they work together. In the following example, from a segment in a course of brief therapy, I want to show how the therapist and patient revise a problem list as therapy proceeds and how they work together on several specific problems.

A 47-year-old woman and I defined the following list of problems by the end of the first session:

1.   A recent grand mal seizure of unknown cause.
2.   Long-standing episodic depressions since death of husband 10 years ago.
3.   Many life changes within past year:
     a.   Move from Idaho to Oregon.
     b.   Quit job.
     c.   Moved from Eugene to Portland.
     d.   Son's recent accident.

Investigation of her seizure was obviously the first order of business since a brain tumor is a leading cause of seizures in people of this age. A neurologic examination was normal, however, as were all other investigations. The probable cause was the antidepressant medication she happened to be taking.

By the end of the second session, we revised and added to her list of problems:

1.   Recent grand mal seizure caused by amitriptyline.
2.   Depression, unipolar type.
3.   A high frequency of self-defeating statements.
4.   Lack of pleasure in her life.
5.   Trouble getting along with her family in Idaho.
6.   No place of her own to live and no job.

I told her during the second session that the repetition of negative, well-rehearsed statements about oneself or about one's future was a common reason for continued depression, that a form of treatment called "cognitive therapy" existed for this, and that I would be happy to teach her about it next week. She told me she had thought about renting her own apartment and moving permanently from Eugene to Portland. In light of her unhappiness, I said that sounded like a good idea. She also said the antidepressant medication helped her. Could she take it at a lower dose? she wondered. I thought she could.

The treatment plan, dictated after the second session, was:

1. Keep track of moods twice a day.
2. Write down any negative or self-deprecating statements.
3. Amitriptyline 50 mg twice a day.
4. Engage in at least one thing she likes doing during the week.
5. Try to find herself an apartment.

She said her mood was up slightly when we met again the following week for the third session. She'd made arrangements to move to Portland permanently. We spent much of the hour talking about the results of her neurologic investigation and her recent discouragement. Her pleasurable event of the week had been a visit from her brother-in-law; they had gone to dinner twice.

She discovered that she frequently repeated two statements to herself: "I'll never find another job," and "I'll never get out of this," "this" referring to her present situation and frame of mind.

Therapist: Is the first statement true?

Patient: It seems like it.

Therapist: I know you're discouraged by this past job, but what about your work record before?

Patient: It was pretty good.

Therapist: And you did several different things?

Patient: Yes.

Therapist: Tell me about why you'll never get another job.

Patient: I don't know.

Therapist: Well, if there's no good reason and your work record is good, why continue to indoctrinate yourself? Can you think of an alternate statement to 'I'll never find another job' which would be more accurate in light of the facts?

Patient: I'm discouraged now because of a lot of things but I have a
good record and I'll probably be able to find another job.

Therapist: Sounds good — and realistic.

The treatment plan for the fourth session was:

1. Continue keeping track of moods.
2. Practice alternate sentence every time she catches herself saying, "I'll
   never get another job."
3. Write down alternatives (one or as many as she chooses) to "I'll never
   get out of this."
4. Continue medication.
5. Continue plans to get an apartment and move in.

She moved fast, and by our fourth meeting she had found an apartment in the city, had practiced correcting herself when she began to think
she could not find another job, and had come up with a realistic alternative
to the thought that she would never get out of her present troubles. Her
mood was also better.

We mutually ended therapy after six meetings. She had not solved all
of her problems, but she had made some important moves and her morale
was better. Notice that the list of her problems was not only different but
also more specific after our second meeting, that I identified her self-
defeating statements as a problem, and that our treatment focused on well-
defined problems.

I sometimes ask patients to collect information or keep some records
for me between sessions. I never use the word "homework" or "assignment" since that sounds like schoolwork and the patient may never have
liked school. If significantly depressed, a patient may keep track each day
of his or her moods on a ten-point scale, where "0" means very depressed
and "10" means very high. If a patient is able to define a specific and
troubling behavior such as lying or hair-pulling, he or she may be asked to
keep track of it for a period of one or two hours during the morning or
evening.

There are good reasons for patients to collect information. I want
them to know that therapy is a collaborative venture and that they are
expected to participate. The information they obtain may also be critical
in identifying and solving a problem.

Counting or keeping records also promotes awareness of the problem.
In up to 20 percent of cases, simply instructing a patient to count the
occurrences of troublesome behavior enhances the patient's awareness of it
to the extent that the person stops it without further therapy![1] Also,

record-keeping gives both the patient and the therapist the opportunity to see whether a particular strategy is working. A written record of a rise in a patient's mood from 3 to 8 in the course of two weeks may itself provide a morale boost.

In the next example, a simple request to collect some information helped a patient answer his own question. He wondered if he was manic-depressive. He could not clearly associate mood swings with particular events in his life. I asked him to keep a record of his mood three times a day and note any specific situations that caused him to feel depressed.

When he returned two weeks later, he said that he had discovered a strong relationship between his pattern of living and his moods. If he drank too much in an evening, if he got behind in his work, if he felt rejected, and if he fought with his girl friend, he ended up depressed. When he exercised a couple times a week, kept regular hours at work, and did not drink too much in the evening, his mood was good. His record-keeping convinced him that he did not suffer from manic-depressive illness.

Sometimes a patient returns for the next appointment and has not carried out the agreed task. There are several reasons. The patient may not have understood what was asked or the reason for doing it, or may have found the task trivial or silly. Refusal may mean that the patient has no investment in changing. When in doubt, be generous. If the patient says that he or she has failed to collect information, the therapist can ask what happened. If the patient lost the paper on which the information was kept, the therapist might ask that the information be recalled as well as possible and then ask, "Would it make sense to try the same thing next week?" The therapist can also ask, "Sometimes people are put off for one reason or another by that kind of thing. Were you?"

The best way to encourage the patient to collect information, however, is to explain at the beginning why such information is important.

Therapist: Let me tell you why I'm asking you to collect some information between sessions. First, it might save us some time. Second, counting can increase your awareness. We often don't realize how frequently we do some things. Third, it gives us both an idea of whether anything's changing or not. One other thing: if you get home and say to yourself, 'What did he want me to do?' please call me.

If the task is complicated, the therapist should ask the patient to call in a few days to discuss any problems the patient may be having with that task. Adjustments can then be made before the next appointment.

Occasionally the therapist needs some piece of information which the patient does not get around to obtaining. If the information is important for the progress of therapy, the therapist may have to say:

Therapist: I feel stuck. You're pretty sure you put people off somehow and you think Sarah could tell you something about how, but you're reluctant to ask her. I know it's hard to ask, for all the reasons we've talked about, but I don't know how we can get past this point without that information.

At other times, the patient does not collect information between session for reasons of preference or personality. When that happens, the therapist will have to think of other ways to approach the problems. Therapists who aspire to help a wide variety of patients must do what the patients' situations call for and not be overly committed to an exclusive way of helping people. Because patients have different personalities and different problems, they obviously require different approaches. Therapists, in fact, should not even assume that all patients who come to their offices want to get involved with problem-solving. For example, a woman recently came to see me because she did not love her husband any more but felt obliged to stay with him, at least for the time being. She had several questions. Are second marriages any more successful than first marriages? What is the impact of divorce on children? What were the chances her husband would change some of his well-established habits? I tried to understand her predicament as well as I could. I shared information with her, asked some questions, discussed her questions. There was no need for anything more specific. In other words, the therapist tries in each and every case to understand what the patient needs, and then attempts to meet those needs. Specific techniques are used if they are likely to help, but it may be more useful to hold them back and instead listen, discuss, share information, encourage, and so on. Don't always be problem oriented!

A beginning therapist may also err by expecting too much of the patient. Getting a job or forming a friendship are tasks of great complexity, for example, and may take a long time. If the therapist chooses to work on either of these tasks with a patient, it is wise to break them down into smaller steps. In order to help one patient get a job, for example, the therapist and the patient broke the task down into the following steps:

1. Places to look for a job — newspapers, bulletin boards, at school, etc.
2. How to call and ask if a certain job is available.
3. How to respond if turned down.
4. How to behave in an interview.

5. Writing a summary of the patient's work record.

The therapist should not assume that anything is easy for the patient. A shy person may find it very difficult to tell an automobile mechanic what repairs are needed for a car. An employee may find it very difficult to refuse for the first time an employer's request to work overtime. Only the therapist sensitive to such difficulty can appreciate the achievement of the patient's first step in a new direction.

A patient may identify a large number of problems. I try to select one or two of the most troublesome. I have found that it is hard to work intensively on more than two problems at a time. The attempt to change too many things at once is an invitation to failure, and every patient needs the encouragement of success. One way to promote it is to start with small steps and a limited number of problems. As patients gain confidence, they solve other problems by themselves.

To define problems and to begin to work on them is one of the hardest stages of therapy. The best beginning is a specific and concrete understanding of problems, and the best way to such an understanding is by asking the patient for specific examples. In therapy as in every task of life, well begun is half done.

REFERENCE

1. Maletzky BM: Behavior recording as treatment; A brief note. Behav Res Ther 5: 107–111, 1974

The Proceedings of Therapy

Some patients can identify their problems and state their goals in the first interview, which makes the transition from the first meetings to the work of therapy easy. Not all patients define their problems or state their goals clearly, however. They tell you they feel discouraged or do not get on with other people but are unable to say why. Other patients are not able to define specific problems because they feel overwhelmed in their present state of mind; they cannot see the trees for the forest. A number of patients will pick unrealistic goals. "I want you to help me so I'll never be anxious again." "I want to do something that will help me forget the past entirely." Others will wish to work on so many problems that a lifetime of therapy would not suffice.

There are helpful approaches in each case. For those who cannot identify the underlying problems associated with, say, a depression, one approach is to seek more information. One woman, discouraged because she had so few friends, learned from an acquaintance that she was left out because she rarely called people on her own initiative.

Patients who feel overwhelmed are usually able to identify their problems more specifically once they have had a chance to settle down in the calming atmosphere of therapy. People in crisis are not themselves. As they pull together, as their emotions come under control, so does their judgment, their perspective, and their ability to think more clearly. The difference between a first meeting with a person in turmoil and the second or third meetings with the same person in control can be exceedingly dramatic.

For people who pick unrealistic goals, a matter-of-fact statement by the therapist is best: "I can't guarantee you'll never feel anxious again, but I can see some things you can do that would help you get your anxieties under better control." To those who threaten to swamp the therapist with problems, I say something like, "I'd like to focus on two or three of the problems you've mentioned. It would be best if we narrowed down. What would be your first two choices?"

Sometimes the therapist and the patient will identify a problem together and set up a plan of treatment, but the patient will not get around to working on it. This often occurs when the patient is not yet ready to confront his or her problems. For instance, one woman knew her marriage was not working and was aware of the reasons why. But she told the therapist that if she tried to change anything, the marriage would crack wide open. She was not ready for that. The therapist had to respect her decision. People may have to live with their problems awhile before they decide to face them. Patients have a right to choose their time to act.

This does not mean that the therapist should never push, however. I push some patients — chronic schizophrenics, for example — only very cautiously. With most patients, my decision to push them to take some action depends on how I size up the situation. I think to myself, "Is this person's situation mainly a matter of choice, change, or crisis?"[1]

A number of people consult a therapist when they have choices to make and feel stuck. The man who cannot make up his mind whether to stay with his wife or divorce her and marry his mistress, or the woman who does not know whether to quit her job and follow her boyfriend to California or continue in her job and run the risk of losing him, are but two examples. Other people have identified specific problems and want to change themselves, for example, the young woman who wanted to stop lying.

A great many people come for help when their plans for living have been shattered by events such as divorce, death, a serious medical illness, or the loss of their job. They feel confused, uncertain about what to do, depressed, anxious. They are not in a position to make choices or changes until their crisis has abated.

When a person comes to me in crisis, I never set a time limit to therapy or push the patient to action, at least at first. If the situation is acute, I use the techniques associated with crisis intervention. I am generous with my time and readily available by telephone; I listen carefully as the patient pours out his or her feelings; I encourage the patient as far as possible not to skip the normal routines of daily living; I am free with my advice and do not hesitate to help in making plans.

But as the crisis resolves, and the need for a patient to make choices or changes becomes more apparent, I'm more inclined to push the patient to action. I give patients more rather than less time before I do this, however. I remind myself that patients are cautious, properly so, about making choices or changes they may be forced to live with for a long time.

When a number of sessions with a patient have gone by and nothing has happened, or I begin to get restless because I know I will hear the same things I heard last week and the week before that, I say something. For example, I had met every week for 3 months with a 43-year-old woman whose husband had left her. Her confusion about what had happened and what she should do now was by no means resolved — this can take months to years — but it had become apparent that she had to take action of some kind. We had talked, of course, about what she needed to do. Instead of taking action, though, she used our sessions to complain endlessly about her husband. Finally, at the end of our 13th session, I said, "You know what steps you have to take in order to get these problems under control. When you've taken the first step with at least one of the three problems we've talked about, why don't you call me back and we'll set up another appointment." I never assume that talking can take the place of action. In fact, talking can become a substitute for action.

When people choose to change something about themselves or their situation, I warn them that most change feels unnatural at first. A person who has trouble getting along with other people because he's too critical and rarely compliments others will not find it "natural" to compliment anyone. Such a person will inevitably return to therapy the following week and tell the therapist how hard it was to compliment others because it felt unnatural.

Change also requires practice and repetition. One should not expect it to occur effortlessly and be established forever in one try. Patients often underestimate the amount of practice that change requires. Behavioral changes are intimately connected with changes of thought and feeling. These should be allowed for, even mentioned ahead of time. These feelings and thoughts toward the behavioral change may be positive:

Patient: I don't like your suggestion that I ask one of the other teachers about how they deal with the problem. But I asked anyway and she gave me some ideas about how I can use my time more efficiently.

But the thoughts and feelings can also be negative; the therapist should be prepared.

Therapist: (to the father of a 17-year-old son) I suspect that as you try to avoid criticizing Bill so often, you'll experience some feelings of anger. This often happens when someone's trying to change. We won't have another appointment for a week, so why don't you call me in a couple of days to let me know how it's going.

And when he calls, the therapist should be braced to hear criticism of Bill, criticism of the program, and, often, criticism of the therapist.

No step is too small when it comes to behavioral change. Programs often fail because people bite off too much at once; they expect that change will be easy and they will be able to change large amounts of behavior at once. This is untrue. Change encounters resistance from two powerful sources. There is first of all an intrinsic resistance to change caused by old, familiar, and ingrained patterns. Secondly, there is the extrinsic resistance to change which comes from other people who expect us to act in the ways to which they're accustomed.

The problems which a patient and therapist agree to work on together can be thought of as the cells of the therapy tissue; the relationship between them is surely the matrix. During each and every course of therapy, a lot of interaction takes place between patient and therapist that is not goal- or problem-oriented. The therapist does a lot of listening, reflecting, paraphrasing, nodding, acknowledging, and questioning. The therapist tries continually to understand the patient in a relaxed, attentive, interested, and natural way. Technical expertise should never interfere with concern, compassion, and humaneness. Comments, observations, and sharing information are all part of therapy. A lot of therapy, in fact, is thoughtful discussion.

The therapist should not ignore the amenities of normal social interaction. I say good morning or good afternoon to my patients. I offer them coffee if I am drinking a cup of it. I make sure tissues are on the table next to their chair. I offer to get them water if their mouth is dry. I darken the room if the glare is too bright and turn up the lights if the room is too dark.

Therapy is always helped along when the therapist stays with the patient emotionally. Part of this is accomplished by making comments that reflect an understanding of the patient's feelings.

Patient: I felt awful when I started crying in front of him.

Therapist: You didn't want to cry but the dam just burst.

In a similar instance, a beginning therapist, in his attempt to make the patient aware of an incongruity between her behavior and her communication when she said she felt awful, asked, "Why are you smiling when you tell me that?" This response was bad. It not only failed to convey empathy, it also moved the interaction away from feelings and, in fact, sounded critical.

In another sequence, the dialogue was:

Patient: I didn't want to tell you about the pregnancy.
Therapist: Why not?

Of course the tone of the therapist's voice is very important here. The response was not necessarily a bad one, but the therapist could have shown more empathy by saying, "It's a hard thing to talk about."

A skilled therapist also moves therapy along by understanding the messages behind the patient's communication. Whether or not these communications should be made explicit to the patient depends so much on context that I hesitate to prescribe when to make them explicit and when not to. At the right moment, however, a proper interpretation of the message behind the message can powerfully move therapy ahead because it communicates understanding and reveals the patient more fully to himself.

Patient: My daughter said I'd fight tigers for her.
Interpretation: ("I'm a good mother. I stand up for my kids.")

Patient: The doctor predicted I'd never get through a third pregnancy, but I did.
Interpretation: ("I've come through in the past against all odds.")

Patient: When people are around and I feel I don't have control, I feel like killing myself."
Interpretation: ("I feel so discouraged about by ability to say no that I can't see any way out.")

Patient: The kids don't eat at all at dinner any more.
Interpretation: ("Dinner has become an unpleasant time in our house.")

A particular statement — as the preceding examples illustrate — may be shorthand for a whole range of thoughts and feelings. To pay attention only to the words or to the behavior is to miss the complexity and meaning that every communication conveys. The therapist must try to grasp and decipher the meanings behind a person's behavior, the messages behind the words.

In trying to understand the patient, the therapist should make good use of hunches and intuitions. These come about when the therapist pays attention to both the nonverbal parts of another person's behavior and to his or her own feelings.

Therapist: (feeling sadness in a woman who's suddenly become silent) Has something just occurred to you that's hard to talk about?

Patient: (suddenly bursting into tears) Yes.

*   *   *

Therapist: I have the feeling you'd like to ask me something and you're hesitant.

Therapist: The way you talk about Jack makes me wonder if your heart's really in the relationship.

Helping a patient achieve a different perspective on a troubling situation is yet another way of facilitating the work of therapy.

Therapist: (to a 40-year-old woman who complained that her husband's physician wasn't paying enough attention to the emotional side of his illness) Yeah, I know what you mean. But I've also wondered whether the only way someone in his position can keep going is to ignore a lot of the emotional side of illness.

*   *   *

Therapist: (to a 22-year-old woman who complained that her boyfriend didn't want to listen to her depressive symptoms). I wonder if he's reluctant because he sees positive things about you, not just depression.

The therapist's ability to recast events in a more positive way can also help because it enables the patient to view a particular experience as an achievement rather than as a problem.

Patient: I did something I'd never done before. I told Frank I was too tired to go to the basketball game with him on Saturday. I felt so awful afterwards.

Therapist: It sounds like you're trying for the first time to set some of your own limits.

Sometimes it is necessary for a therapist to share observations about the patient's behavior. I think this is always difficult (at least it is for me) and is probably done better in group rather than in individual therapy. In a group one person's observations may be corroborated by other members; but, at the same time, the patient will usually have the support of other members of the group. Interpersonal feedback in individual therapy can look too much like criticism if it is not done carefully.

However, when there is evidence that the patient's behavior in therapy is the same behavior that causes trouble with the people in his or her life, the therapist should be willing to take a risk. The issue is easiest to approach if the patient brings it up.

Patient: I wonder if I'm doing anything that makes it hard for people to listen to me?

Therapist: Have you asked anyone?

Patient: Yes.

Therapist: What did you learn?

Patient: Nothing.

Therapist: There's a couple things I've noticed in here that I could tell you about. Several times, while you've been talking, you look away so that it's hard to get your attention and ask a question. Sometimes, too, when I talk to you, you don't seem to acknowledge what I've said, so I don't know whether you've heard me or not.

But if the matter must be brought up more directly:

Therapist: You've said that you don't talk with other people very well. I have observations from this meeting that I could tell you about.

Personal feedback has to be given carefully and tactfully. The therapist should talk about specific behavior and never label the patient. A working therapeutic alliance must be firmly established before this is attempted. I rarely give this kind of feedback to patients in the first few sessions. Sometimes, too, an audio or visual recording of the session, which can be played back to the patient, is invaluable. People are quick to pick up on the tone of their voice, their facial expression, and their posture.

A therapist should not overlook straightforward solutions to problems. One woman got over her phobia of driving on freeways after her therapist suggested that she get the brakes of her car relined. A young man who suffered from very odd episodes of numbness in his legs discovered (after two years of neurologic workups and psychiatric consultations) that his peculiar feelings would disappear if he stood up and walked around. A college student's anxiety about school was markedly relieved when a therapist told her she should not try to study 8 hours a day, only 2. An elderly man's depression was virtually cleared up when the therapist suggested he find someone who could take him shopping twice a week.

The therapist does not need to come up with all the answers, however. Patients often have very good ideas about how to solve their problems. A therapist can often be helpful by encouraging the patient to translate certain ideas into action.

Therapist: (to a 55-year-old woman suffering from unrequited love) Any ideas about how you can get out of this rut?

Patient: I know I've got to get out more and stop thinking about him all the time.

Therapist: How will you go about that?

Patient: I plan to go to the coast this weekend with a friend.

Therapist: Sounds right.

*   *   *

Therapist: (to a lonely young woman) It really hits me how lonely and isolated you feel right now.

Patient: (crying softly) Uh huh.

Therapist: What do you need to help you through this?

Patient: People!

Therapist: I agree. Anyone come to mind?

Patient: Only Dan, and I don't want to get involved with him again.

Therapist: What about people you could call, not only here but also in Seattle?

Patient: Yeah, I have some people I could call.

I also make it a point to reinforce patients when they do take steps to help themselves:

Therapist: (to a woman who has pasted upbeat messages to herself around the apartment) That sounds like a very creative approach . . . .

*   *   *

Patient: I've felt so much better this week. I've done more.

Therapist: Good news.

And sometimes I say to a patient, "I'm as interested in what goes well in your life as I am in the problems. I'd like to know what you've done during the week that's made you happy, what went well with other people, and so on. Let's not neglect that part of your life!"

I want to convey to people that I'm interested in their whole life, not just their problems. It is possible to concentrate too much on problems in therapy, which is bad for both patient and therapist.

Unfortunately, a therapist can erect many barriers to helpfulness. One barrier can be a rigid hypothesis about behavior or treatment. We all have our pet theories that may be generally valid but may not always apply. One of my favorites is that anxiety attacks in married men are often associated with preexisting and hidden marital problems, but I have had to learn that this is not always true.

Other therapists believe that traumatic childhood memories must be exposed and discussed before symptoms will disappear, or that depression represents anger turned inward toward oneself and must be expressed outwardly before recovery can occur. I am skeptical about such firmly held notions. There rarely is only one approach to a problem, and a dogmatic stance about the superiority of one therapeutic approach over another is usually unwarranted.

A barrier can also be created between patient and therapist if the therapist prescribes a type or course of treatment before the patient feels understood. Therapists should not be too quick to prescribe a course of therapy for a patient who is anxious first of all to explain his or her problems.

Therapists can create an obstacle to treatment if they fail to appreciate the amount of psychological distress a patient may be feeling; and of course therapists can create a major barrier to helpfulness if they become overly discouraged with a patient. Therapy can be a dangerous way of making a living. Therapists are not shot in the line of duty very often, but a therapist's morale surely can suffer. Make no mistake about it: hopelessness and depression have a contagious quality. When a therapist is discouraged with a patient, then a consultation with a supervisor, a talk with a colleague, or — as a last resort — a referral to another therapist may be in order. The patient who cannot work successfully with one therapist may work quite successfully with another.

A patient with numerous and formidable problems can also discourage a therapist. This can be a particular peril for the beginning therapist, who may not yet have learned to define a list of problems with the patient and work on one or two of them.

Unwarranted optimism can be a danger, too. Therapists should be careful about setting therapeutic goals too high, which can be a major cause of disillusionment for both patient and therapist. Therapists can usually control their therapeutic fervor if they remember that change usually follows a long and arduous effort, that it is rarely easy, that it is gradual, that it is always a matter of degree, that setbacks are to be expected, and that most changes are not dramatic but are alterations and shifts in emphasis that take place within the continuity of personality..

There are few patients a therapist cannot help in some way. If the therapist cannot or will not meet a patient's request, he or she should at least think of alternatives.

Patient: I'd like you to give me some Empirin No. 3 like Dr. S. did.

Therapist: I don't think that would be wise, but I'd be happy to try something we talked about earlier, relaxation.

                    *   *   *

Patient: (demandingly) I want to see you Monday or Tuesday at four.

Therapist: (evenly) Unfortunately, those times aren't open right now, but I'd be happy to call if I get a cancellation. In the meantime, would any other day do?

The therapist and patient should usually aim at starting work on some concrete issue by the second or third session. There are, to be sure, hazards of focusing down too early: the patient may not feel understood and the therapist may, in fact, fail to understand the larger meanings of the patient's problems. But there are also risks in waiting too long: the patient may feel the therapist cannot get a grip on the situation and so may lose hope and interest; the therapist may allow the treatment sessions to become exploratory and rambling instead of focused and directed.

It is better to be bold than timid. No therapist can pick just the right problem to work on with the patient or inevitably intervene in just the right way every time. The process of therapy is one of choosing, trying out, reevaluating. Even though therapists may choose to work on a particular problem with a patient, this does not mean that they stop listening, talking, and redefining problems as new information becomes available, whatever the stage of therapy. All courses of therapy require flexibility, the ability of the therapist and the patient to adjust to changing circumstances and new realizations.

After the first few interviews, I usually wait for the patient to start the meeting. If the patient remains silent, I might say, "Where would you like to start today?" or, "You look thoughtful." If the patient begins by telling me that he or she feels better, I acknowledge it and often ask, "What did you do?" I like to encourage patients to see themselves as the agent of change whenever possible.

I always make it a point to have looked at last week's notes about a patient before our session starts. This orients me to the session and helps me keep track of what the patient is working on.

If the patient has been working on a specific problem and it has not been brought up by midsession, I do it. I might say, "We agreed last week that you'd tell Bob when you felt angry instead of holding back. How did that work out?" Or, to a person who agreed to keep track of her moods, "What did you discover when you kept track of your moods a couple of times each day?"

Patients usually have more to talk about than just the problems they have defined with their therapist. I welcome that, of course. They want to talk to another human being, not an information-processor. One cannot overestimate the value of talking, the relief that unburdening oneself to another person can bring, especially at the beginning of therapy. Also, as I have already said, new or hidden problems may come up at any time which force the therapist and the patient to change their strategy and tactics.

In fact, there is a good case to be made against too much structure or direction in psychotherapy sessions. There should always be time and room for the free, the spontaneous, and the unplanned. Indeed, this is what makes for interest in therapy, for both patient and therapist. Therapists have to keep an eye on treatment issues, but this does not mean that all their attention has to be riveted there at the cost of spontaneity. Some of the best therapy sessions I have participated in were relative unstructured.

Immediately before the therapy hour, a therapist sometimes is unsure of the direction to take with the patient in that session. This can mean different things. Is therapy at an impasse? Is the therapist preoccupied? If a therapist persistently has these feelings about the session, it is probably a symptom of directionlessness.

Therapy has its ups and downs. There will inevitably be meetings when the therapist and patient feel enthusiastic, ambitious, and well focused; during other meetings they may feel discouraged, slack. There are days when I feel that the only thing worse than a cancellation is a kept appointment, and I am sure my patients have such days too. The realization that these vicissitudes occur is usually enough to overcome them. Neither therapist nor patient should expect the other to be in top form at every meeting. Obviously, if the therapist is ill or too discouraged to carry on, it is only proper to reschedule the appointment.

The number of sessions I spend with a patient in the course of therapy varies widely. For those who come to see me in the midst of a crisis, eight or so visits usually suffice. I have a few patients with personality disorders who have been in therapy intermittently, and some regularly, for several years, and other patients who are not involved in regular therapy but who come to see me when they run into trouble. I also treat a few schizophrenics and manic-depressives whom I plan to see at least intermittently for the rest of their lives. I have always tried to carry a wide variety of patients.

I usually see my patients for 50 minutes once a week, but that also varies widely. Patients in crisis may need to be seen 3 times a week for an hour; other patients may need the boost of a very short session only once every six months. There is nothing sacred about the 50-minute hour; if the patient and I finish our work in less than 50 minutes, we stop. I charge less for a shorter appointment, too.

I believe that I help most of the people who come to see me. I would have left my residency in psychiatry early if I had not felt that one person can help another; my experience as a therapist has now convinced me that this is so.

I realize that with experience I have become more selective in accepting those I can help, and referring elsewhere those I cannot. For beginning therapists success will be harder to achieve if only because they have less control over the selection of patients.

Finally, therapy is not the only way in which a patient's life can be improved. Treatment is not the only way to resolve conflicts. "Life itself," Karen Horney once remarked, "still remains a very effective therapist."[2]

REFERENCES

1. Gilmore S K: The Counselor-In-Training. Englewood Cliffs, N.J.: Prentice-Hall, 1973, p 45
2. Horney K: Our Inner Conflicts. New York, Norton, 1945, p 240

Problems in Therapy

Therapy is unruly. Uneventful courses of treatment are rare; therapy is guaranteed to tax a therapist's intelligence and emotions. No wonder Harry Stack Sullivan said that therapy is the hardest work there is.[1]

Problems may occur so early that therapy never gets off the ground. People who feel coerced into coming or those who have no real faith that a therapist can help may keep their appointments, but anything resembling therapy is unlikely to result. Other people, who are not coerced and who do have faith, find their way to a therapist's office but fail to return a second time. This usually occurs because they do not feel understood. Therapists are not always helpful; some are too busy, while others, having a bad time of their own for any number of reasons, may be temporarily handicapped in their ability to help.

When beginning therapists are unhelpful, it may be because they feel overwhelmed. People who come to therapists want relief, reassurance, new ideas, understanding, and comfort, as well as medicine. They may bring to the therapist the problems of a lifetime. This can be too much for the novice, who may not know even how to define problems, much less do anything about them.

Beginning therapists often respond to their new patients with under- or overactivity. Therapists who become quiet and uncommunicative because they are anxious cause a strain on patients, who may misinterpret the therapist's silence as lack of warmth or understanding. Patients feel reassured when they know their therapist is alert and receiving signals. The therapist should try to relax and act as naturally as possible. A helpful mental image for the therapist is to imagine that he or she is a person talking over a problem with a friend rather than an analyst interviewing a patient.

When a therapist shows anxiety through overactivity, the anxiety takes the form of too many questions, too few paraphrases and summaries, too few empathic comments, too many suggestions, and too much advice. Anxiety also reveals itself when a therapist becomes preoccupied with the patient's past and neglects to focus on current problems, when he or she feels driven to take verbatim notes of the therapy sessions, when the therapist goes overboard and becomes too informal or chatty with patients, and when he or she turns all the patient's questions back on the patient. "Why did you ask me that?" "What do *you* think?" All beginning therapists lose patients as they engage in these maneuvers to control their anxiety. This is usual and expected. Other defenses against anxiety can be more worrisome. Two in particular concern me; these are premature labeling and anger.

LABELING

The more insecure the therapist, the more likely he or she is to label another person with pejorative terms like "hysterical," "senile," "demanding," "manipulative," and other graphic words. Viewing a person exclusively as "hysterical" or "manipulative" makes it difficult to accept him or her with sympathy and tolerance. Helpful understanding is thus thwarted. Labeling also reduces the patient to a category, which diminishes the therapist's ability to relate to the patient personally and in a therapeutic way. Premature labeling can be a mortal blow to therapy. The first step of therapy should always be understanding.

ANGER

A second worrisome sign of insecurity is anger and rejection. This often occurs once the patient is labeled as "dependent," "demanding," or "manipulative." The therapist's annoyance then may show itself in frequent judgmental remarks, a sense of impatience and irritation, and sometimes in angry and early confrontation.

This becomes an unfortunate turn of events, since the patient quickly loses the opportunity to have a "corrective emotional experience."[2] It's bad for the therapist, too, who usually knows that the situation could have been handled more skillfully.

Whatever the stage of therapy, anger can be a problem. Anger is, in fact, the most disruptive emotion in psychotherapy. Learning to manage it is one of the central challenges in treatment.

A therapist's anger is usually aroused when patients ask for too much time or too much support, when they ask for things the therapist does not want to do or does not believe in, when they demand medication, when they become angry at the therapist, or when the therapist is overloaded. Annoyance and anger may also result when a patient presents a vexing problem that exposes the therapist's feelings of inadequacy and incompetence, when a therapist has strong erotic feelings towards the patient, or when the patient reminds the therapist of someone he or she does not like. Therapists may also get angry when a patient does not make progress in therapy, when intentions are not carried out, or when the therapist feels manipulated or conned.

Every therapist, whatever the level of experience, feels angry at patients at times. This is only natural. In fact, the opportunity to work through an episode of anger, whether it arises on the part of patient or therapist, may be a powerful learning experience for both patient and therapist alike. There are important reasons, however, for a therapist to control this anger.

One's judgment is poor in the grip of anger. Things can be said which are not meant and are later regreted. Patients are demoralized anyway, and the last thing they need is something that looks like an attack on their self-esteem. Anger also prevents one from understanding another person, that first goal of therapy.

When I suddenly feel angry about something that's happened in psychotherapy, I've learned to immediately fight back the impulse to express it. I ask myself, "What's going on here?" "What's the patient doing that's bothering me and why am I feeling angry?" I may say to the patient, "Tell me more," as a sort of emergency phrase to buy time while I compose myself. If I can't figure out my feelings during the session, I wait and think about them after the interview. I've found it invaluable to talk about my angry feelings with trusted colleagues or a savvy friend – people who will not just agreeably see things my way but who will take my feelings to heart and talk with me about them.

I also find it useful to remember that patients often come across as angry when, in fact, they feel helpless, discouraged, or vulnerable. One woman, who asked me demandingly what I intended to do about her problems, told me in a later interview that she had felt hopeless about herself; she had concluded that she would not be taken seriously unless she was forceful. A middle-aged man demanded medication at the end of the first interview. He later told me he was worried I'd reject him; he wanted proof that I was willing to help. So much of an individual's behavior that can put off another person stems from insecurity, low self-esteem, fear of rejection, and dread of criticism. These feelings are often expressed by their opposites — demanding behavior, anger, imperiousness, and so on.

I feel angry when patients push me too far, when they demand too much. When I find myself getting to the point of anger, I try to understand why. What do a patient's too frequent phone calls mean? Do they represent an emergency? Is the patient not getting enough of me right now? Are erotic feelings a possibility? Setting limits may be necessary at this point. This is one of the best ways I know to dissipate my anger.

Therapist: (matter-of-factly to a patient who was calling three or four times a week) I won't be able to accept calls from you more than once a week. I need time away from my job, too.

This is true, by the way. A therapist has the right to live his or her own life away from the telephone and away from the office. The confidence to tell a patient this comes with experience.

Anger can be the cause of mistakes at any point in the course of therapy. One beginning therapist, for example, got annoyed at his patient's persistent requests for advice, guidance, and suggestions shortly after the patient's husband had left her. The therapist labeled the woman as "too dependent" in his own mind and told her to come back only if her husband came with her. Talking it over afterwards with his supervisor, the therapist realized that his feelings resulted from a sense of inadequacy — he did not know what to do, not with just this patient but will all patients who asked for advice and support. The supervisor reminded him that almost everyone in crisis becomes more dependent on others, that the patient was not asking the therapist any questions ("What should I do?" "Do you think he'll come back?") that she would not have asked a friend, and that there were ways to handle such questions: answer some of them; reflect the patient's feelings back to her about others, etc. The therapist realized he had shoved the patient out the door. But how could this mistake be corrected, now that the patient believed that she could not return without her husband?

The therapist called the patient and said, "I've thought about our last meeting and realized I was too abrupt. I wanted to see you with your husband for the reasons we talked about, but if he doesn't want to come, I'd be happy to see you alone." The patient thanked the therapist and promptly made another appointment.

Apologies may be in order for some mistakes. For others, the most convincing apology the therapist can make is to behave differently in the future. As an example, a patient of mine called late one afternoon and wanted an appointment that day. She was a demanding woman anyway, who often got angry when she did not get her way. I was tired and bothered by her frequent phone calls. (I had not yet told her what my limits were and was paying for my tardiness.) I told her my earliest next free appointment was three days away. She was silent, which also annoyed me; in our sessions, she often started a conversation, then became silent, which forced me to carry the conversation forward. I was determined not to do it again. She said a later appointment would not work. I remained silent. "Let her come up with an alternative," I thought, in irritation. Then she said, "Okay — thanks," in a discouraged way and hung up.

I was annoyed with her but I could have handled my feelings better, I thought afterwards. My tone certainly conveyed no kindness. It was true that she had a demanding way of dealing with people (something we had been working on), but was it fair of me to expect that she would be able to shed this pattern when she was feeling discouraged? Doesn't a therapist sometimes have to bend a bit more than the patient? On top of it all, I had not even found out why she had called to make the extra appointment. So much for understanding!

In this case I did not call her back since I was pretty sure, from my past experience with her and because of a certain faith I had in our relationship, that she would call again if she needed to. But I brought up the incident early in the next meeting with, "That wasn't a very successful conversation we had, was it? Why don't we talk about it and see what we can learn?"

I mentioned a faith in the relationship. By this, I mean that I had enough confidence in the strength and durability of the therapeutic bond to know that mistakes, errors, tactlessness, differences of opinion, and anger could be tolerated and worked through. I believe that every truly therapeutic relationship conveys a powerful message which goes something like this: "Risks must be taken. I will make mistakes. Differences between us are inevitable. We may get angry, annoyed, frustrated, or discouraged with each other. These feelings do not mean that therapy must end.

These feelings are part of any intimate relationship and should be talked about."

If a patient becomes angry with me in the course of therapy, I ask why. The feedback I have received from patients has not always been pleasant to hear but most all of it has been valuable. One patient said he felt I did not care about him when I was late for his appointment. Another told me she quit therapy because she felt I took her husband's side in an argument. A third told me that I sometimes gave her double messages and showed me what she meant. Honest feedback from anyone is unusual. I have learned to appreciate it from my patients.

PUSHING A SINGLE APPROACH

A beginning therapist is not helpful if he tries to force a particular idea or course of action on his patient. It may be better to be tentative, especially at first. For example, a young woman tells a story that makes the therapist wonder whether the unexpected death of her mother (when the patient was nine years old) has something to do with her current problems. What should not be said is, "It's clear that the loss of your mother is behind your problems. We'll have to work on that first." Much better to say, "I wonder if losing your mother didn't have something to do with what's going on now?"

A 40-year-old man comes to therapy because of marital problems, and the therapist concludes that he could profit from couples' therapy. But the therapist should not say that this is the only road to salvation, especially upon learning that his wife has no intention of coming with him. Instead, the therapist might say, "Couples' therapy could help, I think, if your wife were willing to come in. But if that's not possible, we can work together in other ways." A therapist who pushes one idea or approach to a problem too insistently usually pushes the patient right out of therapy.

ROUTINE

Therapy can also bog down when a patient and therapist have agreed on a course of action that turns out to be unhelpful or wrong. The therapist should be alert to this if therapy is not going anywhere. A patient and I had agreed that her obesity was handicapping her socially and emotionally. She had unsuccessfully tried a variety of weight reduction programs before.

It became clear to both of us after several weeks that out plan was not working. Her response was to cast about for another program. My response was to raise a question:

Therapist: We've assumed that it's your obesity that's restricting your life. Is it possible that we've got it backwards, that your eating habits are somehow a result of your restricted life? If that's true, maybe the best thing to do is to get out and do more. Maybe that will give you the incentive you need to lose weight. At any rate, we've tried the other idea and it hasn't come to much. What do you think?

It is easy to get into a routine with a patient. Both the therapist and patient can become wedded to a particular way of doing things which dulls the therapist's sensitivity to changes in the patient and to new problems. A woman and I defined one of her central problems as a well-established either/or style of dealing with other people. Of her boy friend she said, "If he doesn't come over tonight, I'll never call him again." Of her supervisor she said, "If she doesn't say something good about my presentation next week, I'll quit." We worked together on ways she could relate more flexibly to her boyfriend and to her supervisor. But one day, in the middle of the session, it dawned on me that something was wrong. She was telling me of several recent incidents that she had not handled well, and which illustrated her old problem. I found myself thinking irritably, "If only she could try harder." I have learned to regard that sense of irritation as a warning. Then, suddenly I realized what was happening: my concept of the situation was so fixed that I was failing to hear what she was telling me now, that she was lonely, isolated, flirting with suicide. I removed my mental blinders and acknowledged her feelings.

UNDERSTANDING EXPECTATIONS

Failure to ask patients about their expectations of therapy often leads to problems. There is no reason to assume that what the therapist thinks the patient needs is what he or she wants. The therapist must ask. When listening to the answer, the therapist has to decide whether he or she can meet the patient's request.

Therapists should not turn down too quickly a request that sounds unreasonable. The patient's request for help may be hard to interpret. Many patients do not know what therapy is about and others have unrealistic expectations:

Therapist: What would you like to get out of therapy?

Patient: I'd like to be just like Frank wants me to be.

Obviously, a therapist should not say, "That's impossible. You can't be his Pygmalion. Besides, it's not healthy." Instead, the therapist's thoughts may be as follows: "Interesting problem, unusual request. I wonder what her husband is like, I wonder what she's like, and what their relationship is like." The next response might be

Therapist: What kind of person would he like you to be?

A 50-year-old woman was having intermittent chest pains because her lover would neither commit himself to her, nor leave his wife.

Therapist: What do you want most from treatment?

Patient: I want to be able to accept the situation as it is and not have these pains.

Therapist: Okay. Anything else?

Patient: I need someone to talk to about the problems I'm having. I feel so lonely.

Therapist: All right.

In this case, the therapist was better able to help the patient with her second request than with her first. The therapist has some latitude in choosing what to respond to.

PATIENTS' NEEDS

Misunderstanding a patient's needs is another problem for a beginning therapist, who is sometimes too oriented toward change as the only goal of therapy. With some patients this orientation is perfectly appropriate; they want help to change this or that behavior. But they may also come for other reasons.

I find it helpful to think about the choice, change, or crisis categories that I mentioned in the last chapter. Therapy must fit the patient's needs. A therapist who insists that a patient change when the patient really needs help making choices is behaving like a physician who insists on treating a patient for heart failure when the patient needs treatment for kidney disease.

A patient who cannot decide what to work on in therapy can be a problem. When this happens, a therapist's impulse is to pick the problem for the patient. It can be so easy to see what the patient should do! This is usually a bad move to make, however, and the therapist soon realizes that as a result he or she now has more invested in therapy than the patient. This is not the proper configuration.

If a person cannot decide what to work on, I try to understand why. It may be, for example, that his inability to commit himself to any course of action is the problem. Therapy then has a focus. But if a lack of commitment to action is not a general problem and the patient has trouble only in the therapy session, one way to handle it is as follows:

Therapist: I know that making a decision about what you want to work on is a problem, but I don't know where we can go unless you do. I obviously can't select your goals for you. Why don't you think about it for a couple weeks and give me a ring. If you decide on something, we can always get together.

An inability to select a goal in the first place is one problem. To lose sight of the goals as therapy proceeds is another. The therapist may experience a directionless, disoriented feeling as therapy proceeds, and wonder what is being worked on with the patient. When this happens, I sometimes use a simple and helpful reorienting procedure.

Therapist: Let's pretend for a minute you're coming to see me for the first time today. You come in, sit down, and I ask you what problems you'd like to work on. How would you list them at this point?

LACK OF PROGRESS

Slack periods often occur in the course of therapy. A limp session or two does not worry me. It may be important for the patient to be able to sit quietly, not to feel pressured to talk, not to make decisions, or not to work on problems. Therapy does not always have to be packed with action. If several sessions go by and nothing seems to be happening, however, I raise questions about what the goals are, what we are doing, whether we have a grip on the problems, what the person's feelings are about therapy and about me, and so on.

Therapy may come to this kind of impasse when the patient withholds important information which they may be embarrassed by, they do not know the importance of, or they are not ready to accept the consequences of divulging. I recently met with a couple with whom I went absolutely nowhere in our sessions together. In the fourth session, the husband told his wife that he was having an affair with another woman. As a therapist, you have to wait for this kind of information, but if I suspect the patient has a secret, I may ask whether something's on his mind that's hard to talk about. Or if he looks preoccupied, I might say, "You look as if you're thinking about something."

When patients fail to make progress in therapy it is often because they are afraid that they will lose the therapist if they improve. In many cases like this, the relationship with the therapist has become more important to the patient than the therapy itself. The weekly meeting with the therapist is the high spot of the week. The patient has selected the therapist for a friend without giving the therapist a choice in the matter. The implicit hope these patients have is for indefinite therapy. I, for one, am not willing to do that. I bring the matter up if therapy seems to be going nowhere.

Therapist: I have the impression that things have been moving pretty slowly in here. How would you like me to help you at this point?

A person usually refers back to the original problems. If I sense a willingness to work, I'll set aside more sessions. If nothing happens after several more meetings, I may say, "Is it possible that our meetings together each week have become more important than solving any of the problems you're working on?" Whenever this happens with women (in my case, since I'm a male therapist), I have to consider the possibility that the patient has romantic or erotic feelings toward me. Romantic feelings toward the therapist range, in intensity, from mild to severe. If they are mild and nondisruptive, a discussion of them may not be necessary. When romantic feelings are intense, however, they must be discussed; paralysis of therapy will otherwise result. These can be extremely difficult feelings indeed to talk about. If they are not talked about, however, therapy will not move forward. In my experience, romantic feelings are most likely to occur when the course of therapy is long rather than short, when the patient is lonely, and when the patient has a borderline personality.*

One way to approach these feelings is discussed in the last chapter of this book. Briefly, the patient should be encouraged to talk about the

---

*When I diagnose this condition, I use the new DMS-III criteria.[3] These patients show an affect of anger or pervasive loneliness, have a history of turbulent personal relationships characterized by an alternating pattern of aloofness and overdependency on others, show marked mood instability, make frantic efforts to avoid being alone, and so on.

romantic feelings and fantasies, which are always entertained more freely in isolation than in company. The therapist should try to understand why they occur, and avoid being put off or alarmed by them; nor should the therapist become cold and aloof. Instead, these feelings should be discussed, and the patient should be made to understand why the therapist cannot get involved in this way. The therapist's own verbal and nonverbal behavior should be consciously scrutinized in order to avoid leading the patient on. If single, or involved with marital problems, the therapist should be especially alert to this possibility.

Intense romantic feelings toward the therapist are never easy to manage. Their occurrence is not rare, however, and the most intense cases can assume psychotic proportions. This has happened twice in the past five years; in both cases I tried to work through these intense feelings with the women involved, but the results were disappointing. In both cases, the women did much better with other therapists after I arranged for referral.* Erotic and romantic feelings may also arise when patient and therapist are of the same sex, of course, but I believe the principles of management are similar.

PERSONALITY DISORDERS

Patients with personality disorders usually come to therapy in the midst of a crisis. A low tolerance for stress is characteristic of people with personality disorders, in fact.[5] Crisis intervention techniques are of course called for when patients decompensate under stress. But no matter what the type or length of therapy is, the therapist must always appreciate the great fact of personality and, to some extent, tailor the therapy to fit the patient's style. Experienced therapists do this almost intuitively. They have learned how futile it is to exhort an obsessive person to relax and enjoy life, or how frustrating it is to ask a person with a hysterical cognitive style to keep records.

The topic of personality disorders is far too large to be discussed extensively here, but I at least want to make a few remarks about the ways a therapist can recognize and approach a few of the more common personality problems.

---

*Ernest Becker, in his brilliant book *The Denial of Death*,[4] has written an important chapter on the dynamics of the transference phenomenon. Every therapist should read it in order to appreciate the power and complexity of this problem.

Hysterical Personalities

Patients with a hysterical personality have trouble being specific, which makes it hard for therapists to work with them in a focused way. Instead of giving specific information, hysterical patients will report their feelings with "It was awful!" or "It was wonderful!" They have trouble sticking to the point. They exaggerate their symptoms: "I vomit every ten minutes." "I lost sixty pounds in two weeks." The cut and colors of their clothes are eye-catching. When therapists attempt to sum up the session at the end of the hour, they find themselves at a loss for details. Hysterical patients often idealize and flatter the therapist: "I felt so much better after our meeting." This may feel good to the therapist, but it means nothing as far as outcome of therapy goes. Patients with a hysterical style often have many physical complaints, and ask freely for advice.

If a patient with a hysterical personality style has many physical complaints, one has to think of Briquet's syndrome, a disorder characterized by multiple physical complaints in multiple organ systems.[6] Briquet's syndrome is stable over a long period of time. Patients who have it are very difficult to treat. In spite of a therapist's best efforts, it can be impossible to get them away from talking about anything besides their physical symptoms. They can be frustrating with their vague symptoms, their demand for extra time and attention. Few of them referred for psychotherapy persist in treatment.

For patients with well-established hysterical personalities, with or without Briquet's syndrome, supportive therapy is usually the treatment of choice. Some patients with this diagnosis can work in a more specific way, however. With them, I gently refuse to accept vague descriptions of their interactions with others, for example. Instead, I consistently ask for specific examples of what was said, who said it, what was said in response, etc. Such patients are liable also to leave their own behavior out of the account. But with practice, such patients can be brought to see the part they play in the problems they have with other people.

Obsessive-Compulsive Personalities

At the other end of the personality spectrum, in style and substance, are the obsessive individuals. When asked for information they provide too much detail, which can be frustrating. Their preoccupation with details reflects not only their need to be complete but also their need to be in control. Obsessives have high standards for, and often feel critical toward, themselves and others. They may obsess about their own lack of worth, and a therapist's reassurance rarely helps. When they decide to direct their critical beam on the therapist, it can get pretty hot. Progress, they say, is too slow; the therapist is not doing enough. A problem-oriented approach, they suggest, is trivial. And, in spite of all this, they are reluctant to take new steps on their own behalf for fear of failing.

In the first interview with an obsessive person, I listen, but by the second or third interview I become more active, sometimes by interrupting. When they begin to wind themselves up with details, I may say, "Let's get back to the question I asked a minute ago." And then I repeat the question. When the person has a list of copious notes and I can clearly see that we will only get a quarter way through them before the end of the hour, I say, "Time, unfortunately, is short. Could you select just a couple of the problems that bother you the most so that we can spend more time on those?"

When obsessive persons are in crisis, they typically try to *do* more – more work, more rearranging, more ritual – in the attempt to regain a sense of control. It does not work. Instead, they feel even more frantic. I often point out to these individuals that, to be truly effective at anything, one must allow for breaks from the routine. Being a good mother or, say, a good pianist, also means spending time away from one's role or work.

I try to use the obsessive person's own need for structure in a therapeutic way. My suggestion to one man, who was involved in ever more frustrating furniture-arranging rituals, was to engage in his rearranging for 20 minutes three times a day, then leave the house. This maneuver did not cure him but it helped. Another obsessive man, a biochemist, was spending more and more time at his office but getting less and less done. We decided that he would practice leaving at 5:00 P.M. sharp no matter what. Knowing this, he began to use his time more efficiently and was actually relieved to leave at the time we agreed upon.

Schizoid Personalities

Schizoid individuals, who are emotionally blocked, isolated, and aloof are hard to relate to. They do not trust people and their alienation may wear the mask of arrogance. They often complain of emptiness and loneliness but have trouble telling the therapist what part they play in their unsuccessful interactions with others. They also complain of joylessness.

Schizoid individuals often feel overwhelmed by the distance between themselves and others but, at the same time, are disdainful of a therapist's attempts to break down their interpersonal problems into smaller steps that might allow for progress. They complain that the work of therapy is not taking place on a large enough scale. These individuals are also much better at intellectualizing than at taking action.

For this reason, schizoid people can be frustrating to therapists who are action-oriented; therapy is always slow and always tedious. Change, when it occurs in these individuals, is a process of slow steps, of "grinding labor."[7] I often ask what emotions lie behind the experiences and events they report — "How did you feel when that happened?" Schizoids are very guarded; they doubt themselves profoundly; they often fear their inner feelings and would like to disown them. Merely describing their feelings in an atmosphere of acceptance may be the first step toward accepting themselves.

I listen carefully to what they tell me about their interactions with other people. Their reports, if one listens intently enough, can yield invaluable information. From one schizoid man, I was able to learn that he never initiated a conversation with anyone else in the course of an entire week. When he finally did it successfully, we spent the following hour talking about the experience. In addition, I ask about feelings when I notice small changes in the person during the interview. For instance, if a person scowls and looks sad for a second, I might say, "You scowled when you said that." This has to be carried out judiciously, of course; you don't want to be too intense and scare the person away. What I hope to convey to the patient sooner or later is that he has feelings which show, that emotions are not necessarily dangerous, and that the ability to show some feeling can be important for maintaining relationships with other people.

Paranoid Personalities

Patients with paranoid personalities, who are suspicious, guarded, mistrustful, and cold often cause aversion in the therapist because of their argumentativeness and rigidity. A therapist should never confront paranoid patients with their irrationalities too early in therapy. Paranoid individuals live in a world of suspicion and opposition; their paranoia is not just a symptom but a way of life. They require two things: patience and more patience. I attend to what they tell me, of course, but that does not mean I agree or disagree when they tell me their suspicions about other people. As I get to know the paranoid person better, and as he or she comes to trust me, I may begin to wonder aloud if there is not another way of looking at a situation or if it is possible that so-and-so acted for this or that reason instead. The patient may disagree, but that does not mean he or she will not think about my comment.

It also helps to pay attention to aspects of the paranoid patient's life which aren't so infected with a paranoid flavor. It is important to remember that therapy often helps most when the therapist focuses on the healthier parts of a person's character. If a paranoid man tells me of a good experience with someone else, I may remark that he sounded thoughtful or sensitive.

I have discovered that many patients with a paranoid personality are surprisingly anxious to stay in therapy, even when the initial sessions with them have been pretty bumpy. As in the case of most personality disorders, you should not expect dramatic changes. Small changes in perceptions and in interactions with others are the marks of successful therapy.

Borderline Personalities

Patients with borderline personalities have many of the characteristics of patients with schizoid personalities: aloofness, emotional isolation, trouble with relationships, low self-esteem, and so on. They tend to become overinvolved with anyone they get close to, including the therapist. Sexual fantasies about the therapist at the very beginning of treatment often suggest borderline psychopathology. They have a hard time working on specific issues because they want an intense, involving relationship, not just some approaches to their problems in living. When they do not get what they want, they may become angry or make a suicide attempt.

Individuals with borderline personalities inevitably provoke strong feelings from their therapists. They can be an immense amount of trouble. They often anger the therapist by their own anger, their unreasonableness, their demands. They often feel empty when the therapist leaves town, and their suicide attempts, carried out while the therapist is on a vacation or attending a meeting, are enough to dampen most homecomings. I have learned to my sorrow how poorly borderline patients tolerate separation. When I plan to be gone from the clinic, I tell these patients about my plans well in advance, listen to their feelings about by absence, and make sure they have someone to call if they find themselves in trouble.

I have probably learned more about myself and about therapy from borderline patients than from any other group of patients, but I suggest that no therapist take on more than one or two at a time unless he or she

is exceptionally hardy. The intensity of their demands, the pain and loneliness of their existence, and the questions they raise about the meaning of
life can be overwhelming.

Any therapist who accepts for therapy a patient with a borderline personality had better be prepared for turmoil, provocation, and stimulation.
Many get into treatment because they are misdiagnosed as depressed,
anxious, hysterical, or schizoid. Some of the therapist's most intense thinking will take place around borderline patients.

In every case with borderlines, I try to keep a focus to therapy; this
serves as a rudder in what often are turbulent seas. The therapist should be
willing to spend a good deal of time talking with the patient about his or
her feelings toward the therapist. Angry, hostile feelings are common, as
are erotic fantasies. If these emotions are ignored or glossed over, the patient will often express them through suicide attempts, drinking, or sexual
adventures. Not all of the therapy session should be spent talking about
feelings, however. The borderline, like all other patients, has problems in
his everyday here-and-now life which are worth attention.

For example, a 30-year-old woman with a borderline personality said
she was lonely and isolated. In the course of therapy, we discovered she
had some well-developed thoughts and behavior patterns that kept people
away from her. She was a person who never started anything on her own.
"If people cared, they'd call me first," she said. She could not set her own
limits with men when they asked her to go out for an evening, to go hiking,
or to go to bed. Disgusted with herself and furious usually with the men
who "exploited" her, she coped by withdrawing. Her reactions to arguments with people were unusual. When she found herself at odds with her
boyfriend and he threatened to leave her, her first thought was of suicide.

These are not simple problems, admittedly, but it is possible to approach them in psychotherapy. There is a difference, after all, between the
very difficult and the impossible. At one point or another in the long
course of therapy, we worked on each of the problems I mentioned;
though we rarely had smooth sailing together, we met with a modest degree
of success at the end. Of course, we talked about many of her feelings toward me and many of my feelings toward her. No doubt this helped the
course of therapy. But our success in narrowing down on some specific
problems was also very helpful, as she told me later.

Sooner or later the therapist almost always has to set limits with his
borderline patients around such issues as the frequency of phone calls, the
number of appointments, the use of medicine, the scope of therapy, and
the extent of the therapeutic relationship. The therapist may also be

forced to tell the patient how much angry, destructive behavior will be tolerated and exactly what steps will be taken if a suicide attempt is made. Borderline patients may need to have limits set for them; they often behave very unreasonably. One woman tore down the curtains in one of our clinic offices; another had temper tantrums in the waiting room every week. Limits help provide the structure and coherence that disorganized people need. Limit-setting also helps the therapist control his or her own anger and frustration which, if left unchecked, will lead to rejection of the patient. Setting limits can be difficult because borderline patients often practice a subtle form of emotional blackmail. In effect, they say, "If I can't have what I want, then there's no reason to live and I'll commit suicide (and you know who'll be responsible)." The therapist must have the courage to tell the patient what the therapist can and cannot do, what will and will not be tolerated. If this is done firmly and reasonably, the patient often settles down in treatment.

Borderline patients, like many schizophrenics, do not possess the "vital lie of character" which helps to buffer most of us from the assaults of life.[4] The delicate web of meaning, wound so assiduously around us from birth until it becomes part of our character, has not been wrapped so tightly around borderline people. Consequently, the abyss of meaninglessness and chaos is closer to them. Sometimes, if the therapist lets down his or her guard, their despair, their profound loneliness, touch to the core. There is nothing to say. In fact, at such moments there is no need to do anything. This is the time to stay and be.

PREOCCUPATION WITH THE PAST

In the first few interviews, a patient will occasionally ask what kind of therapy I do. I usually ask them if they have a particular kind of therapy in mind, which tells me something about their expectations. I often go on to add that I do many things in therapy. Sometimes I listen, sometimes I want to know about past events, sometimes I pay attention to behavior, sometimes I'm interested in how events are experienced, and sometimes I advocate a course of action.

In the course of therapy, patients may ask how they came to be the way they are. Many people ask this question out of curiosity after they have made some progress in therapy. They wonder how their childhood experiences have shaped their lives as adults. I may say, "It's a good question. Why don't we spend a few sessions talking about it and see what we can come up with." Most people do not insist on a total reconstruction of their early lives. They want a plausible understanding of how they came to be what they are. One man, for example, who had originally come for help because of nonassertiveness, wanted to know how he had become so timid in the first place. We talked for three sessions about the personality of his mother and father and about his interactions with them. He concluded that his timidness developed because his mother so often criticized him.

A smaller group of people who want to delve into their past are pre-occupied with it to the exclusion of their current problems. This preoccupation can be their way of avoiding the current problems.

I have mixed feelings when these patients tell me they want to spend a lot of time on their past. Two patients I have seen in the last 8 years wanted psychoanalysis, as it turned out, and I helped them find an analyst. I have asked the others, who wish to stay and pursue the matter, what particular traits or patterns they hope to elucidate by an exploration of their history. If I have reason to believe that their desire to pursue their past may represent an avoidance of their present, I may ask, "What's your idea of how an understanding of the past will help you with the present?" On occasion this question has shifted therapy back to the present. If it does not and they seem bent on their exploration, I may offer them several sessions in which to talk about their past. In about a quarter of the cases, the patient and I come to a working notion of how their past has affected their present. In another quarter, the patient loses interest.

The other 50 percent of these patients continue to be preoccupied with a reconstruction of the past. If this is what they really seem to want and I do not see the point to it, I may try to refer them to a more analytically-oriented therapist. If they do not want to do that, I can be pretty blunt with the patient:

Patient: I can't get a grip on the basis for my problems. There's no co-herent explanation.

Therapist: What form would a coherent explanation take?

Patient: I don't know. (This was his usual response.)

Therapist: I think you may be on the wrong track. From what you've told me, I think your present behavior and attitudes are what are getting you in trouble.

If that does not steer therapy back into the present, I may say that I am feeling stumped about where to go and that perhaps it is time to take a break from treatment.

MEDICATION

Some patients will ask for medication if the therapist is a psychiatrist. This usually comes up early in therapy. I listen carefully to those requests; many, if they are for lithium or antidepressants, are reasonable.

I have more trouble with patients who ask me for a minor tranquilizer such as Valium or Librium. The main reason for prescribing these drugs is to help a person control anxiety during a stressful time. I do not hesitate to prescribe these tranquilizers when I think they will help, but I tell the patient that I will not prescribe them for longer than two or three weeks. I go on to explain that: they tend to lose their effect so that the dose has to be increased for the same effect; some people report they cause a lowering of mood; the drugs themselves may cause confusion or drowsiness, particularly if the patient is older.

These are the easier cases. The harder ones consist of people whose physician, months or even years before, prescribed minor tranquilizers for them. They have been taking the drug ever since, gradually increasing the dose, and have come to rely on it; many will ask for a refill. At this point I want to learn why the drugs are necessary and whether anything else might help. I also ask the person how long they believe they will need them. But then I usually hesitate. Some of them notice this and ask, "Are you reluctant to prescribe it?"

This is one of the few times in therapy I may give a lecture. Assuming that I am not convinced they need the drug, I tell them why I am hesitant. I also tell them that I appreciate that they feel anxious, but suggest other ways the condition might be managed: by relaxation, through feedback, or by modification of the situation which leads to nervousness, if possible. If they have been taking medication for several months, however, I realize that it is not advisable or easy to stop abruptly, even if they are on relatively low doses,* so I tell them I'm willing to prescribe the medication for another two weeks, after which I'd like to work with them on reducing the dose down to zero. I warn the patient that he or she may experience more anxiety during the withdrawal period but that those feelings, too, will pass.

If the patient still wants medication for anxiety after the prescription of minor tranquilizers has run out, I may consider a course of low-dose tricyclics. A recent report suggests that this is a promising treatment for chronic anxiety.[8]

*Any person who takes over 100 mg of Valium a day for several months should be considered a candidate for a serious withdrawal reaction.[9]

MISSED APPOINTMENTS

Missed appointments are inevitable in the course of therapy. Patients usually have good reasons for missing appointments: misunderstanding about
the appointment time, illness, trips, etc. I do not charge for missed appointments since I can always use the free time. If a person misses several appointments within a short period, however, it indicates some negative
feelings about therapy. I invite the patient to talk about them:

Therapist: You've cancelled several appointments in the last five weeks.
             You've told me the reasons, but I wonder if you have some
             feelings about therapy that we haven't talked about yet?

More than once the patient and I have had a discussion about missed
appointments and I have assumed the problem to be under control. Then
another cancellation occurs. When that happens, I may have to say, over
the phone or in person, "I don't see how therapy can go forward without
regular meetings. If you have to miss again, I won't be able to reschedule
further sessions."

UNPAID BILLS

Some patients don't pay their bills. They may come once or twice, quit
therapy, and disappear. Clinic patients (as opposed to private patients)
will then receive monthly bills and reminders to pay. Private patients
receive a polite reminder the first month. ("May we hear from you regard-
ing this account? Thank you.") The second missed month my secretary
calls the patient personally. At the third month, I let them know that I
will reluctantly have to turn over their bill for collection by a certain date
unless I hear from them soon.

Some regular patients allow the bill to lie unpaid for a long time. I
have been tempted to tell every patient in our first meeting that I set a
limit to the amount of credit I extend: 300 dollars. I do not do this, however, because I want to convey the impression that I trust that the person
will pay the bill. The majority of my private patients are very good about
paying so I feel my policy is justified.

If the bill mounts steadily toward the 300-dollar limit (or goes over)
and no payments come in, I bring the matter up.

Therapist: My secretary reminded me that your unpaid bill is two hundred and ninety dollars. Will you be able to make some arrangements for payment?

In the majority of cases, this is enough. The person will usually express some surprise that the insurance company has not paid or tell me why no payment has been made. Many write out a check for a partial payment on the spot. If I feel the answer is vague, however, or still feel worried that a payment will not be made, I tell them that my policy is not to make another appointment if the outstanding bill is over 300 dollars.

Setting limits is not easy to do. All of us in the helping professions feel a twinge of guilt when we have to withdraw our help, however much the move may be justified. But to ignore unpaid fees and missed appointments is as unwise as it is impractical. Neglect of these issues often reflects conflicts within the therapist about money and time. The beginning therapist often feels he or she is not worth the money the patient is being charged for the session, or may feel hesitant to bring up tardiness or missed appointments for fear of precipitating a confrontation with the patient and thereby exposing his or her own anger toward the patient.

There are no neat and ready solutions to the common problems of therapy. The therapist who wishes to learn how best to deal with them will continue to think about them and struggle with them, will read about them whenever possible, and will of course ask more experienced therapists how they manage them.

REFERENCES

1. Sullivan HS: The Psychiatric Interview. New York, Norton, 1954, p 10
2. Alexander F: Current views on psychotherapy. Psychiatry 16: 113–122, 1953.
3. DSM-III Draft: Diagnostic and Statistical Manual of Mental Disorders. Washington, D.C., American Psychiatric Association, 1978, pp K-20–22
4. Becker E: The Denial of Death. New York, Free Press, 1973, pp 127–158
5. Lion JR (ed): Personality Disorders. Baltimore, Williams & Wilkins, 1974, p 246
6. Goodwin DW, Guze SB: Psychiatric Diagnosis (ed 2). New York, Oxford University Press, 1979, pp 70–87
7. Yalom ID: The Theory and Practice of Group Psychotherapy (ed 2). New York, Basic Books, 1975, p 384

8. Jobson K, Linnoila M, Gillam J, et al: Successful treatment of severe anxiety attacks with tricyclic antidepressants: A potential mechanism of action. Am J Psychiatry 135: 863–864, 1978
9. Shader RT (ed): Manual of Medical Therapeutics. Boston, Little, Brown, 1975, p 196

Ending Therapy

The therapist and patient should end therapy when the original therapeutic contract is fulfilled; when the patient experiences a relief of symptoms and feels an improvement in living; when nothing is happening; when the patient is getting worse rather than better; when the patient moves away or feels he or she cannot afford therapy; or when the therapist plans to leave the clinic.

Occasionally the patient and the therapist will agree quickly on a goal at the beginning of treatment. This usually involves relief of a specific symptom, like persistent tightness in the throat, or a phobia or a tic. The therapist meets with the patient a certain number of times (which may be set in advance) and it becomes obvious to both of them that therapy has helped.

Therapist: (to a patient with an animal phobia) It sounds to me as if your problem with animals is pretty much over.

Patient: Yes, it is. At least I hope so.

Therapist: Are there other ways I can help you right now?

Patient: Not that I can think of.

Therapist: Okay. Maybe this is the time to stop meeting regularly. There are a number of ways we can go. We can set aside an appointment for three weeks or so, you can phone me in a week or two and set up something, or you can simply call me in the future if you wish. Which would you like to do?

Patient: Why don't I just call you in a month or so. Would you have time if I wanted to make another appointment?

Therapist: Of course.

Most of the time, however, therapy does not end so neatly, with the initial complaint solved. Improvement is usually a matter of degree. A 28-year-old woman who suffered from obsessive ruminations found that she was less troubled by her symptoms as several therapy sessions went by. There were two reasons: A man with whom she was having trouble moved away, and a low dose of haloperidol helped reduce the intensity of her troubling thoughts. Another patient, a 38-year-old woman who worked full-time, felt less depressed after several family conferences were held and the family agreed to share more of the burden of housekeeping and cooking. The end of therapy came about like this:

Patient: I'm really feeling better.

Therapist: That's good news.

Patient: I appreciate what you've done.

Therapist: Thank you. But don't forget to give yourself some credit. I didn't invite your family in, for example, *you* did.

Patient: I know.

Therapist: While we're on the topic of therapy, I wondered how many more sessions you'd like.

Patient: About two.

Therapist: Okay.

Patients are more or less explicit about the ways therapy has helped them. They may say, for example, that role-playing, encouragement, or just talking matters over in therapy has been helpful. The therapist may appropriately get some credit for these changes, but the wise counselor will also remember the large role that fortuitous events play in a person's life which can affect the course of therapy so profoundly. One woman, for instance, had a drug experience with LSD that helped her accept the loss of her husband. A middle-aged man was more or less forced to move from a small town to a larger one and found that his abdominal pain, which had bothered him intermittently for years, was better. He attributed it to getting away from his mother, though his relationship with her had not even been identified as troublesome before. A very withdrawn man was notified that a short story he had written had been accepted for publication, an event that enhanced his self-confidence to the extent that he went out and joined the world again.

In summary, therapy should end when a patient's initial complaints or symptoms are resolved or alleviated and when the patient feels an improvement in living.

Therapy should also end when nothing seems to be happening. The therapist may see a patient week after week, and listens to the same story again and again. The therapist has usually made attempts to get the patient working in therapy but sooner or later concludes that therapy has turned into chat. This can be a dangerous time in therapy because the therapist may be tempted to rationalize the absence of direction and focus. A 52-year-old woman, for example, who complained of an unhappy life and a dominating husband, failed to make any progress in therapy. The therapist thought to himself, "It's hard to justify seeing her, but since I'm the only one she can talk to, the appointment at least gives her a chance to get out of the house. She cannot seem to take any steps to enlarge her circle of friends but who else will she have to talk to if not me?"

This can be an unfortunate rationalization. Weekly conversations may actually retard a patient's progress by keeping the level of discomfort just below the threshold at which he or she might take action. All therapists know patients who unexpectedly took major steps when the therapist went out of town, for example. If a therapist begins to feel that he or she has become a purchased friend to the patient, this should be discussed and a decision should be made whether to continue therapy.

Sometimes a patient seems to feel worse, not better, as therapy proceeds. He or she will complain that thinking and talking about the problem actually makes it worse. This is not common, but I have seen it happen twice in the past 10 years. When it occurs, I try my best to understand why. If the patient's feelings persist, I may encourage him or her to stop, suggest a referral elsewhere, or invite the patient to call me back to talk at another time.

Therapy may end because the patient plans to move away. If he or she wishes to continue treatment, I do my best to obtain a referral in the new location.

Occasionally patients will want to stop therapy because they can no longer afford it. If I know something about the patient's financial status and I am surprised by the news, I wonder if it is not a tactful way of telling me he or she would like to quit therapy. I may ask about it.

If money is a genuine problem, I consider reducing the fee, but I first ask the patient what he or she would like to do. Some say that they would like to come back when they can afford therapy. Others ask if we cannot continue meeting, but perhaps less often or for shorter periods. I usually agree. Sometimes, too, patients' requests to stop are a way of saying that they cannot afford interminable therapy. Setting a termination date may be the answer.

Treatment ends also when the therapist leaves the clinic. Most psychiatry residents come to the outpatient clinic for 6 to 12 months. Whether or not the therapist brings up the matter with the patient depends on how long the treatment is likely to last. If it is brief therapy, there is no reason to mention it; if the therapy is likely to be longer, the rotation change has to be brought up.

Therapist: (end of first meeting) As a resident, I'll be working in the clinic another five [or whatever the figure is] months. Whether I'll be able to continue meeting after that isn't clear to me right now — it'll depend on my other responsibilities, my next rotation, and so on. I don't plan to leave you in the dark, though. Within another month or so I'll know better what my schedule will be.

The patient often knows when therapy is at an end. I have been surprised how often both the patient and I have become aware of this simultaneously, either because the goals of therapy were more or less reached or because nothing was happening.

Occasionally, the patient will want to stop therapy unexpectedly. I try to understand the reasons why and may suggest one or two more meetings to talk about it. But if the patient insists, I honor the request and rarely try to talk him or her out of it. But I leave the door open in every case:

Therapist: If something comes up or you want to come back, please call. I'll be here.

An occasional patient will quit therapy without telling me beforehand. If I am concerned, I will make a telephone call. I may say, "Mr. K., this is Dr. U'Ren. I didn't hear from you about our last appointment and I thought I'd call to see how you are." To patients who have no telephone I may write a brief note, inviting them to call me if they wish. I make no attempt to contact patients I'm not concerned about.

Whether or not therapist and patient reach the original goals of therapy depends, of course, on what those goals were in the first place. Most beginning therapists tend to be a bit too ambitious for their patients. Goals are important in therapy because they provide a sense of direction for patient and therapist. But most patients stop therapy when they feel better and more in control of their lives, not when a therapeutic contract has been fulfilled. This may be discouraging for beginning therapists, who may even blame themselves for their inability to help their patients accomplish more. It is true that, with experience, therapists broaden their knowledge of ways to help patients; but they also become more aware of their own limitations. They continue to care about their patients, but their egos are not as invested in whether their patients change or not as younger therapists' egos are apt to be. They recognize that their powers are limited by the patient's personality and circumstances, as well as by their own personality and circumscribed knowledge of how to best help people. "Our duty," wrote the philosopher Amiel in 1856, "is to be useful, not according to our desires but according to our powers."[1]

I make it a point to cover several issues as therapy is ending. I often say to the patient, "Let's review how you and I saw your problems when we first met." I may then ask, "How do those same concerns look now?" I also ask patients what they thought helped in therapy, what might have helped more, and whether anything we (or I) did hindered them. Some patients mention a specific technique the therapist used, or a particular comment the therapist made, that was helpful. Other patients will be less specific and will thank the therapist for his or her support and willingness to stick by them while they were going through a bad time.

I also look ahead with the patient. Is there anything on the horizon of the patient's life that we should discuss? If some approaching problem is similar (it usually is) to one we have worked on in therapy, it can be talked about now. Anticipatory guidance is never as specific as one would like, but patients have told me it helped.

I invite people to call me in several months to let me know how they are doing, but I never make this obligatory. About 20 percent do; but there have been patients about whom I was extremely curious or concerned, so I called them. I have never had the feeling they were offended — quite the contrary, in fact — but I still find myself hesitant. I do not want to be intrusive or stir up the memories I suspect some people would rather forget.

In spite of my own cautiousness about this, I believe that we should pay more attention to follow-up than we do. Almost every time I have followed up on an ex-patient, I have learned something that has changed my practice. I have learned whether I have helped or whether I have hindered my patient; sometimes patients will tell you about their feelings only after time has passed. I have learned that most patients with emotional problems have remissions and exacerbations. I have learned that my fellow therapists may succeed when I have failed, a lesson which serves as an effective antidote to the unpardonable belief that if I cannot help a person, no one else can either.

Patients find salvation in a variety of ways, either inside or outside therapy. I have seen people whom I considered hopeless make the most amazing recoveries. Both pessimism and optimism on the therapist's part can prove to be misplaced; in therapy as in the rest of life, the future is never certain.

REFERENCE

1. Amiel HF: Amiel's Journal. H. Ward, (trans). New York, Macmillan, 1923, p 134

Workouts

Blue Woman

I was working in my office one afternoon when I received a call from a man who asked me if I would see his wife. He said she had become dissatisfied with her psychiatrist. I told him I would be happy to see his wife; as a matter of professional courtesy, however, I wanted to talk first with her therapist. I asked the man to call his wife's therapist, tell him that they were consulting me, and ask him if he would call me. This was done the next morning, and I agreed to see the woman later the same afternoon. I asked her husband to come with her.

I learned that Mrs. Moody* had felt depressed for three months. She complained of a lack of energy, poor memory, and trouble making decisions. She often found herself standing in the middle of the kitchen vacillating about which ingredient in a recipe to add next. She compared herself unfavorably with her friends: "They've all done something with their lives. I haven't." She had crying spells, woke up at 4:00 in the morning, and had trouble going back to sleep. Her appetite was poor, and she had lost 8 pounds in the last 2 months.

Therapist: Have things ever gotten so bad during the last two months that you've thought of ending it all?

Patient: Oh, no. I don't think I'd commit suicide no matter how bad I felt.

*All of the names in this and in subsequent case illustrations are fictitious.

There was no family history of depression, but the woman said she had been depressed twice before, the first time 3 years ago, the second time a year ago. Her second depression had responded to antidepressant medications prescribed by her internist.

It was obvious that her symptoms — sleeplessness, trouble concentrating, difficulty making decisions, and her poor memory — were bothering her exceedingly. But there were other things, too.

Therapist: Are there any other things that are getting you down?

Patient: My husband. He feels he can't go any further in his job and he's unhappy. He complains all the time. That gets me down. Then he found out he has to have an operation later this year. I don't know what we're going to do for money.

Therapist: Anything else?

Patient: My son called yesterday from New York and said that he wanted to bring his girlfriend home for Christmas. I just can't face it the way I'm feeling. But if I tell him she can't come, it'll ruin Christmas for him and for all of us.

Her husband had come with her to the interview, and I invited him to come in and talk with me alone.

Therapist: How do you see her problems?

She was starting to go through menopause, he said. Her last period had finished just before her depression began. Also, she missed their children. An oldest son had started graduate school several months before her depression came on, and their daughter was away at college. He also thought his wife was especially hard on herself because she had not pursued a career, though he admitted that he had never encouraged it. He said that she had lately been fretting almost constantly about money in recent months, though they in fact were reasonably well off.

I learned from Mrs. Moody that she had grown up in a stable and secure family. Her parents had been married for 40 years. Her mother was a warm, consistent, and rather controlling person — that combination that is likely to produce a person who is well-behaved, thoughtful of others, able to apply herself steadily, but who may also lack the confidence to express warmth, assert herself, or show imagination.[1] And, indeed, the patient had a personality characterized by conscientiousness, punctiliousness, fretfulness, orderliness, conformity, and a tendency towards self-doubt, probably reinforced by her husband's bad temper, which flared whenever she challenged him.

But in spite of her current problems, she had considerable strengths. She had one intimate friend in whom she could confide; except for her two previous depressions, much milder than the present one, her mental health was good and her physical health, her physician told me over the phone, was excellent. She had not held a job in the work force for 20 years, but her work record during the 5 years she worked after college was exemplary. She had high intelligence and a marked ability to solve problems, especially the practical problems that come up in any household.

Mrs. Moody was an attractive woman of 52, with a high forehead, brown hair with a small amount of gray in it, and strong, chiseled features. She was dressed neatly in a yellow knit pant suit. She sat comfortably and talked easily; she was very articulate. But she looked worried and anxious. She kept asking me why she felt the way she did and wondered if her depression would ever end. She occasionally smiled, though wanly. Her recent memory was normal (on formal testing), but she complained of her inability to concentrate and to remember recent events.

I thought that I could help her with her depression, though I felt a bit apprehensive about her impatience. Would she quit therapy if her symptoms did not go away quickly? I wondered.

After I felt that I had gained some understanding of her problem, I said:

Therapist: You and your husband have mentioned several problems that are getting you down. In what order would you like to work on them?

Patient: I want to feel right, first! I can't stand this trouble I have making decisions. Also, I've had a lot of trouble sleeping. But the only place I feel safe is in bed. Can you help me?

Therapist: I think so. I know how crummy it must be to feel the way you do right now. Let's suppose, though, that you do feel better after a while. Would there be anything else to work on?

In rapid succession, Mrs. Moody mentioned how discouraged she felt about her husband, about her son's girl friend, about the coming Christmas holidays, and about herself.

The problem list that I constructed with her was:

1. Symptoms of depression: sleeplessness, trouble concentrating, low mood, loss of appetite, lack of energy and anxiety
2. Marital difficulties associated with

   a. The unpredictable critical behavior of her husband, which lowers
      her self-esteem
   b. His frequent complaints about his work
3. Apprehension about the coming Christmas holidays
4. A pervasive feeling that she's wasted her life vocationally. She wants to
   find a meaningful job in the future

My assessment was that she was suffering from a moderately severe
and recurrent mood disorder, a depression. I doubted that the problems
that she and her husband had told me about were entirely responsible for
causing her depression, but it was not hard to see that her depression was
aggravating her problems.

It was also clear to me that she required medication for her depression; she was too depressed to work effectively on any of her other problems. I prescribed 75 mg of amitriptyline and told her about the side
effects; the dose was raised to 200 mg per day within 2 weeks. I told her
that she should try to get out of the house at least once a day and that she
should try to exercise several times a week. I encouraged her to visit friends
twice a week but not tire herself doing so. I told her that her depression
would lift sooner or later, probably within 3 weeks, and that, hard as it
might be to imagine when she was feeling so badly, she would not feel
depressed forever.

She had asked me to call her daughter, and after our first meeting I did
so. When I talk to a patient's relatives, I usually tell them how I size up the
situation and how I intend to proceed with treatment. I often make suggestions about ways they might help, ask them if they would be willing to
come in and talk to me if necessary at a later time, and invite them to ask
any questions they may have.

Daughter: What do you think is wrong with her?

Therapist: (to daughter) I think your mother's depressed.

Daughter: What causes it?

Therapist: Several things, I suspect. The troubles she and your father have
              bother her. He can be critical, and that gets her down. I think,
              too, that this is the first time that you and John [her brother]
              have been away from home so long. She's invested a lot in you
              emotionally and I suspect she gets lonely when you're not
              around. I also think that she feels she doesn't have enough to
              do; she has a lot of time on her hands. There's a lot about
              depression we don't understand but we know that depres-

sion isn't uncommon in someone her age. Do you see things at home that get her down?

Daughter: Oh yes, my father really puts her down sometimes.

Therapist: What does she do when that happens?

Daughter: She usually doesn't say anything, but I can see it bothers her.

Therapist: Does she say anything about it to you?

Daughter: Sometimes.

And later in conversation:

Daughter: My brother thinks she's putting on, that she should just pull herself out of it.

Therapist: I think she would if she could. Coming out of a depression is more than a matter of will power. I think that she's at a point where she needs help.

I saw Mrs. Moody weekly and talked to her briefly on the phone up to three times between visits. A month after our first meeting she told me she felt better. Her mood had brightened and she had more energy, but she still had trouble with concentration and memory. I reassured her that she would continue to improve. Since the holidays were approaching and she was still worrying about them, I suggested we make some plans:

Therapist: What do you think will get you down over the Christmas vacation?

Patient: My husband and son will expect me to do everything.

Therapist: Everything? Can you explain?

Patient: Cook all the meals, do all the shopping, entertain.

Therapist: Can you tell them you're not up to it, that you need help this year?

Patient: I don't want to ruin Christmas. I feel like I'm just making excuses. Why can't I just pull out of this? I feel it's a weakness.

Therapist: If it were that easy, you probably would have pulled out of it long ago. Listen, what do you need help with most over the holidays?

Patient: I just can't make all the meals myself. If they could get breakfast and lunches, I could handle the dinners.

Therapist: And would they be willing to do shopping sometimes if you help them make out a list?

Patient: Yes, I think so.

Therapist: Show me how you're going to ask them to help.

Patient: I can't. Why can't I just get over this?

Therapist: If you had a broken leg and it was in a cast, would you have any trouble asking for help?

Patient: No.

Therapist: Well, what's the difference? Is having a depression less honorable than having a broken leg?

Patient: I guess not.

Therapist: Okay. How will you ask for help?

Patient: I'll just say I need it.

Therapist: Show me. Pretend your husband is sitting beside you in the empty chair. How would you ask him?

I often ask patients to show me how they will carry out an intention. I have learned not to assume they can do it effectively without some practice beforehand. Role playing and discussion of a concrete situation can be very helpful.

With her husband's and her children's help, Christmas went smoothly. About 7 weeks after our first meeting, I asked her if she still had trouble with her husband. She said that she had, and wondered if anything could be done about her marriage. But she also warned me, "He's always been the way he is. I don't think he'll change."

Therapist: You may be right, but if he's unhappy with the way things are now, he might be willing to change in at least some small ways that would improve your life together. Is it worth a try or would you rather not?"

Patient: I guess I'd like to try it.

I met with her and her husband for two sessions; both of them agreed they had problems. He admitted he was discouraged about his job and knew that his complaining bothered his wife. He said he often did not show her how much he appreciated her. He did not thank her when she cooked a good meal, for example. He also said that he and his wife had trouble reaching agreement on many issues. He would make a decision after she had told him she couldn't make up her mind, and then she would disagree with his decision. She, on the other hand, said that his temper was the major problem in the marriage for her.

During our second meeting, I got the impression that Mr. Moody was impatient. I was tempted to make a comment about it, but I decided on another course instead:

Therapist: Do you see any connection between the problems you've told me about and your wife's depression?

Husband: Some, not much.

Therapist: What are your ideas about what would help your wife the most?

Husband: I think she should get out more and she should look for a job if that's what she wants.

Therapist: Would you be willing to encourage her if she decided to do that?

Husband: Yes.

Therapist: (turning to Mrs. Moody) What do you think?

Patient: (relieved) I think that would be the place to start, too.

At that moment I was faced with a decision. Should I confront both of them with my idea that at least some of her depression was caused by her marriage? I thought that her husband was denying the role he played in the genesis of his wife's problem. His wife went along with him because she was too timid to disagree. Or should I go along with the patient and her husband, leave the marital problems alone for the time being, and encourage her to do more with her life, perhaps to seek work?

I chose the second course. For one thing, I reasoned, she and her husband might be right. There are many ways to a better life; improving the marriage was only one. If she felt more self-confident, she might also be in a better position to stand up for herself at home. Also, I thought, I could help her expand her life. If that worked, fine. If not, and if information became available that suggested the marriage was getting in the way, I could always see them again as a couple and work with them on their marriage.

At the next session, Mrs. Moody and I began talking about ways she could expand her life.

Therapist: Where would be the best place to start?

Patient: I think I'd like to get back to work sooner or later, but maybe a volunteer job would be best for me right now.

Therapist: Any ideas?

Patient: Yes, I have a neighbor who once offered to help me.

Therapist: Okay. Other thoughts?

Patient: A financial analyst once offered me a job. I could look him up.

Therapist: (nodding) If you want to look into psychology again, I know a clinical psychologist, a woman who's made a career of it, who'd be willing to talk to you.

Patient: But I get so nervous when I think about going back to work, I haven't done it for 20 years.

Therapist: I know what you mean, but it seems to me that you're still at the stage of gathering information. You don't have to commit yourself to anything yet.

Patient: I guess you're right.

Therapist: As long as we're brainstorming together about whether you might look into other volunteer jobs, have you considered looking in the paper?

Patient: I could.

At the end of the hour, I summed up:

Therapist: So there are a number of directions you can go. You intend to talk to your neighbor, ask the person who once offered you a job, look in the paper, and call the clinical psychologist I mentioned. Do you want to do all those things before we meet again next week or do you need a longer period?

Patient: It's up to me now. Two weeks would be better.

Two weeks later she returned and said that she had called everyone except the financial analyst. She had decided that his kind of work did not interest her. Another two weeks went by, and she arrived at her appointment with a *curriculum vitae* in hand. She said she was ready to start looking more seriously for a volunteer job.

Patient: I've been out of it so long, I hardly know what to ask in the interview.

Therapist: Well, what would you like to know about the job you're interested in?

Patient: If there's a chance of working half-time, if there's someone around I could ask questions of when I don't know the answers.

Therapist: All sounds reasonable. Would you like to run through your first telephone call? I could be the employer and . . .

Patient: No, I couldn't do that.

Therapist: Well, would it be easier if I role-played your part at first and you were the employer?

Patient: I think it would.

After 20 minutes of role playing and discussion, we switched roles so that she played herself. A month later she landed her first job in over 20 years, as a volunteer one day a week.

This case illustrates first of all how important it is for the therapist to have a knowledge of descriptive psychiatry so that he can correctly identify the condition from which a person is suffering. The presence of a severe depression should always cause a clinician to consider the use of medication in treatment. The antidepressant medication prescribed for this woman no doubt played a large part in her recovery, but the medication was not, and should never be, the only treatment. This case also shows how important it is for a therapist to define related problems and work on those too. A specific technique – role playing – was helpful.

In the course of therapy, I twice asked the woman to show me how she would carry out her intentions. Patients often underestimate the skill it requires to translate an intention or an insight into action. By asking them to show you what they would do, the therapist creates the opportunity to assess the adequacy of the behavior and to make suggestions for improvement.

Talking to Mrs. Moody's husband and daughter provided me with useful information. It also gave me the opportunity to enlist them sympathetically in her treatment. The support and help of her family no doubt contributed to her recovery.

This case also illustrates how important it is for the therapist not to push a particular hypothesis too hard, i.e., that marital therapy would be necessary for her to recover from her depression. There are always various paths to a better life. In this instance, Mrs. Moody's success in obtaining a volunteer job was one of them.

REFERENCE

1. Becker WC: Consequences of different kinds of parental discipline, in Hoffman, ML, Hoffman, LW (eds): Review of Child Development Research, Vol. I. New York, Russell Sage Foundation, 1964, pp 189– 199

An Anxious Man

A 29-year-old man was referred to me by an internist who wanted to know if there was a psychological basis for his patient's anxiety attacks. The physician had treated the man's symptoms unsuccessfully and wanted to know if I could help. I said that I would be happy to see the patient and asked the physician to have him call me for an appointment.

His problem had begun 7 months earlier. He had been out with his wife and some friends, and they had been drinking. Afterwards, while sitting around his living room, they began smoking marijuana. He suddenly experienced an episode of panic. He felt that his head was getting larger, that his heart would stop, and that something awful would happen to him. These symptoms continued the next day, then occurred the next day and the next. In fact they had continued to occur right up until 3 weeks before our meeting. Episodes were also marked by shortness of breath, palpitations, vertigo, and numbness and tingling in his hands and feet; they occurred several times a day, in different circumstances, and they seemed to have no identifiable cause. During this time he had consulted several physicians without relief. One of them had prescribed Valium, but this only caused him to feel more depressed and he had stopped taking it regularly. Then, unexpectedly and mysteriously, the symptoms stopped. He was relieved, of course, but decided to keep his appointment with me because he had not felt "normal" since his panic attacks. He constantly felt fatigued, unmotivated, restless. He said, "I have to be busy all the time, otherwise I get depressed."

At our first interview, I listened carefully, giving him my full attention, thinking about his symptoms. Could his panic attack of seven months before have been caused by the marijuana he smoked? This is not uncommon. But could the effect have lasted so long? Were there other things going on in his life that might have prolonged his symptoms of anxiety? Anxiety attacks often occur when a person is having trouble with a marital partner. Disappointment and friction at work can also be responsible, but not as commonly as marital trouble. Yet he had not mentioned his wife, which, perhaps, was significant.

Well, after 20 minutes the interview was still young. Instead of asking him right then about his wife and his job, I decided to ask about something he had just mentioned:

Therapist: And what happens if you sit around instead of keeping busy?
Patient: I think about things.
Therapist: Like?
Patient: My marriage.

The marriage, his second, was 5 years old. He had moved in with his present wife shortly after he had left his first wife, after 3 years of marriage and one child. Now the second marriage was going sour. He felt that his wife could not really be trusted. She often had lunch with her boss, a prominent businessman in town, and if she went out to dinner with other people, she did not come home until 1:00 in the morning. On top of this, she was consistently critical of him and was often irritable. Also, she told him she was not interested in sex. On nights when she stayed out late, he could not sleep and would drive around looking for her. He told me some of her specific complaints about him, also: that he had no ideas of his own; that he was jealous and possessive. Two days before, she had suggested they think seriously about a separation. Since then he had been very cautious with her, worrying that if he said anything to displease her, she would leave. He had asked her if she would see a marriage counselor with him, but she replied, "No, and don't turn your psychiatrist into a marital counselor either."

I asked him what else was happening in his life. He said he could not concentrate at work. His job was not in danger, but his supervisor would no doubt notice his inefficiency if it lasted much longer.

I found out very little about his past history in our first meeting, only that he got married when he was 20 because his wife was pregnant, that he had served in the Army during the Vietnam War, that he had been a good athlete in high school, and that he now played handball regularly.

He was a well-built, athletic person about 6 feet tall, weighing 175 pounds. He was dressed in a sport coat, a print tie, and a light-blue colored shirt. He looked discouraged, especially when he talked about his marriage. I liked him and thought we could work together.

The problem list I constructed in my head by the end of the interview was:

1. Marital problems.
2. Anxiety attacks, probably associated with marital problems.
3. Difficulty concentrating at work.

My formulation was:

The patient is discouraged. His marriage is going bad, he doesn't want it to end, and he doesn't know what to do. It sounds as if his wife is almost out the door. I suspect he's expressing his unhappiness through his body and through his anxiety and depression. He strikes me as an action-oriented man who is not practiced in expressing feelings. As often happens, his discouragement and his symptoms are interacting in a negative way: as his discouragement grows, his symptoms become more severe; as his symptoms become more prominent, he feels more discouraged. His trouble concentrating at work reflects his preoccupation with his marriage. His usual way of living, which as far as I can tell seems regular and modulated, does not seem to be aggravating his current problems, but he doesn't seem to have intimate friends and may not have anyone to talk to when he finds himself in trouble.

On the other hand, I think he has a number of assets. He works regularly and gets along well with colleagues. His health has been good. He has a wide circle of acquaintances. He leads a balanced life and exercises regularly. He has above-average intelligence.

Toward the end of our first meeting, I summed up what he had told me.

Therapist: It sounds as if several things are going wrong. Your marriage worries you a lot. You're really uneasy about it and don't know what's going to happen, but you want very much to keep it together. On top of that, you've had these episodes of anxiety until recently and you're worried something's physically wrong with you even though the doctors haven't turned up anything. You told me that you still don't feel back to normal even though the anxiety attacks have disappeared. You've also said that you can't concentrate as well as you'd like at work. Does that say it?

I believe, as does Harry Stack Sullivan, that the patient deserves something from the therapist during each interview.[1] A concise summary powerfully conveys a message of understanding. In addition, I let him know how I looked at his problem:

Therapist: I wouldn't be surprised if there's a relationship between your feelings about your marriage and your anxiety. It's well known that feelings can emerge in the form of body symptoms and it's certainly striking that your anxiety has been most bothersome during the period of time that you and your wife have been having trouble.

And just before the interview ended:

Therapist: It sounds to me as if things are pretty unstable right now. The instability won't last, I'm willing to bet, but that doesn't make it any easier for you. Since your marriage is the big thing on your mind, maybe we should talk more about it next time. If your wife changes her mind about coming, I'd be happy to see both of you together. Otherwise, the two of us can talk and see where we can go.

Most therapeutic efforts should be two-pronged. The therapist and the patient should attempt to deal directly with the patient's troublesome symptoms, whether they be anxiety, depression, paranoid thoughts, a phobia, or the like. One should never scoff at symptom relief, since the successful removal of a symptom in itself increases the patient's sense of confidence. But when symptoms are imbedded in the context of an unsatisfactory life, as they usually are, the patient and therapist should work to improve the patient's life in whatever area — the marriage in this case — is troubled.

He returned the next week. Matters were still very bad between him and his wife. He had not said much to his wife all week and was still afraid she would get angry with him.

Patient: I think she must be having an affair. Why else would she stay out until one o'clock?

He then marshaled evidence to support his suspicion.

Therapist: I think I know how you feel — those suspicions are always painful — but I can't help but wonder how concentrating on that will help you solve your problems with her. Your real goal is to keep the marriage together.

Patient: Yeah, you're probably right.

Therapist: Well, where shall we start?

Patient: I keep thinking I'll tell her she's won, that I can't stand it any more, that it's time we break up.

I recognized this as a desperate all-or-none approach to his problems.

Therapist: That's one way, but there may be others.

Patient: I can't think of any.

Therapist: You told me it's a strain living with the feelings you have. What about telling Sharon about them?

Patient: I don't know if that would work.

Therapist: Neither do I, but we are in possession of valuable information: we both know what's not working.

Patient: That's true.

Therapist: Do you want to try it or are we barking up the wrong tree?

Patient: I don't know how to do it.

Therapist: Let's try it together. Have you heard of role playing?

Patient: No.

Therapist: If we were to role play you and Sharon, I'd take your part or Sharon's and you'd be yourself or Sharon and we'd imagine ourselves in a situation, say, at home. Just to give me an idea of how Sharon would act, why don't you play Sharon and I'll be you. I come into the kitchen at five o'clock and you're sitting there. What would happen?

We spent the next 20 minutes role playing and discussing how he could talk to Sharon about his feelings. It quickly became apparent that he was not used to talking about feelings and was easily thrown off the track if his wife criticized him. I pointed that out, and we practiced ways he could handle it. He left, determined to try the new approach. He also said he might ask his wife to come to our next meeting. We did not schedule another appointment because we thought it might look too prearranged to his wife if he asked her to come in with him and it turned out the appointment had already been set up. He said he would call me after he talked to her.

A month later, he came to see me alone. For reasons he did not understand, but for which he was very happy, his marriage had taken a turn for the better. He could not attribute the change to what we had done in therapy. During the past 3 weeks, his wife had been more friendly, attentive, and loving. Their sex life had picked up. She now told him where she went in the evening and what time she would return.

Therapist: You look happier than when we last met.

Patient: I am. So why is my anxiety back?

His symptoms had returned. But this time he had made some observations which took the mystery out of them. They came on him a day before he took a civil service examination, about which he was apprehensive, and on which he suspected he did poorly. He also experienced anxiety symptoms — dizziness, a sensation of warmth all over his body, numbness around his mouth, and small "explosions" in his head — when he met friends of his wife.

Therapist: What kinds of thoughts do you have when you're with one of those friends?

Patient: Like I'm not measuring up.

Therapist: Do you feel that way right now? Do you have those feelings in your body even as you talk about it here?

Patient: Yes.

He then told me that he still felt very shaky about his wife. Though she had changed, he still did not have a good idea of how she spent many of her evenings. Five days before, for example, she had taken some cookies to her boss shortly after dinner and did not return until 11:00. He was very angry but dared not show it. He had also discovered, incidentally, that he had symptoms when she got angry at him, and he wanted to avoid symptoms at all cost.

Therapist: That's a bind, isn't it? You're angry as hell but afraid to say anything. If you do, you're worried she'll leave you, and if she just gets angry at you, your symptoms will come back.

It was apparent, as the hour neared its end, that his marriage, not his symptoms, was what still concerned him most. Besides, he could manage his symptoms, he told me, either by ignoring them or by taking a very small dose of Valium. At the end of the hour, I asked him:

Therapist: How can I be of most help to you at this point?

Patient: I might be able to talk to Sharon now that we're getting along better. I'd like to try.

Therapist: It certainly sounds as if things are better. I hope you can talk to her. But if that doesn't work or if something else comes up, why don't you call me?

Patient: I will.

As he was leaving, he said, "It feels good to come and talk to somebody about these problems."

Karl Menninger says somewhere that the ability to listen is the greatest therapeutic tool. That, and giving the patient a chance to talk, can hardly be overemphasized. To be able to speak your heart in the presence of a nonjudgmental person who understands you, and who you feel is on your side, can have a tremendous impact on morale.

He came back to me 6 months later. His marriage had continued to improve. He felt that he could trust his wife again and no longer felt jealous. But he could not specify why these changes had taken place.

He still felt anxious at times, but the episodes were less frequent and he was able to live with them. The major problem at the moment was stiffness in the back of his neck. As we talked, he was able to tell me when and where the stiffness occurred: when he was under pressure at work and stayed at his desk too long, occasionally when he was around superiors, and, also, when he was in the presence of his wife's friends.

Therapist: Sounds like some things are a pain in the neck.

Patient: (smiling) I guess that's one way of putting it.

Therapist: It seems to me we can approach this in at least a couple ways. You've recognized several things that seem to cause the stiffness in your neck — when you stay in one position too long at work, when you don't take a break, when you're around the boss, when you're around some of your wife's friends. We could look at those situations and see if we couldn't come up with some ideas about how to handle them differently. Maybe it's a mistake, for example, to stay at your desk for more than an hour at a time without a break. There's another way that we can go, too. I could teach you something about relaxation. A number of people with complaints similar to yours have found that helpful.

It had occurred to me that this was a man who was very sensitive to sensations within his body. This trait made him look a bit hypochondriacal, but perhaps this acute awareness of his body would also allow him to profit from relaxation. Since he was by nature an action-oriented person, I wondered if giving him something to do in order to control his symptoms might not work better than just talking.

I taught him a standard relaxation technique in three sessions. I asked him to practice four or five times a day, for about five or six minutes each time, between our meetings. He found relaxation helpful. When he returned for his second session, he told me, "I never felt more relaxed than I did after our session last week. I almost felt back to normal." He felt no stiffness in his back nor did he experience anxiety episodes. At the beginning of our third session, he said that he had started to feel some anxiety on several occasions at work but he had been able to abort it by relaxing. He said, however, that he now felt much better than he had in a long time. We agreed to discontinue therapy.

This case demonstrates that the symptoms of anxiety can be the patient's ticket of admission for medical care and psychiatric attention. When the therapist accepts the ticket, however, he does not know what he is getting into. He may see a one-act, one-character drama or a production with a cast of thousands. About all the therapist knows at the beginning of therapy is that a symptom or group of symptoms often reflect a patient's unhappiness with a major part of his life.

This man's marriage was in trouble. I believe that I was helpful to him by attempting to work on his relationship with his wife even though she refused to come in herself. Even though I, too, suspected that she might be having an affair, I showed restraint and did not voice the suspicion. That, after all, was not the point of our consultation. The man came to me not to establish whether his wife was having an affair, but how he could get rid of his symptoms and how he could make his marriage last.

I tried to show this man that therapy is a collaborative effort. I told him at one point that I had no answers to his problems but at least possessed the same information he did: we both knew what was not working. There was no reason to continue these unproductive efforts. Why not try something else?

I agreed to temporarily discontinue therapy after our first three sessions in spite of the fact that there was still unfinished business. The patient said that he wanted to quit and see what he could do by himself. A therapist is well advised to honor that kind of request.

This case also shows that the use of a simple behavioral technique, relaxation, can be helpful in relieving symptoms of anxiety and tension.

REFERENCE

1. Sullivan, HS: The Psychiatric Interview. New York, Norton, 1954, p 17

A Troubled Woman

Therapy is rarely a tidy affair. At least not in my hands, or in the hands of several other therapists I know well, all of whom I consider to be exceptionally competent. Case reports from both the psychoanalytic and behavioral literature often give the impression that patient and therapist proceeded in an orderly fashion from point A to point B to point C and so on to happy termination. I suppose this occurs sometimes, but when it does the patient's problem must be unusually circumscribed.

More often, and this is especially true if therapist and patient work together over an extended period of time, therapy demands that the therapist use different approaches for different problems at different times.

My next example illustrates some events that took place during a 15-month intermittent course of therapy with a 35-year-old woman who said, in the first interview, that she had recently been feeling "sad." She was thinking about breaking up with her boy friend, a man she had been seeing for 3 years. But she had doubts about permanently severing her relationship with him, and wanted to talk about those doubts.

She had been divorced 8 years ago. Her husband was the one who wanted out, for reasons she never understood, since she had felt no dissatisfaction with the marriage. Then for 3 years she lived with another man for whom she felt no sexual attraction.

She said that she had always had problems with self-esteem. She felt unsure about herself when she talked with men who seemed better educated than herself. She was dissatisfied with work. She was employed as a managerial assistant to an official in a school system. The work was boring.

Within 20 minutes of the beginning of the first interview, I was able to say:

Therapist: You've mentioned several problems, but from the way you've talked, it sounds as though problems with your boy friend are bothering you the most right now.

Patient: Yes.

Therapist: Can you tell me more about it? Are there specific times or situations in which you feel especially unhappy around him?

Patient: Yes, when we try to talk. I don't think I can stand up to him.

Therapist: Has that happened in the last week?

Patient: A couple of nights ago we were out eating. I'd said something about graft in the police department. He said it was a stupid comment.

Therapist: What did you say?

Patient: Nothing.

A specific example like this enables the therapist to get a handle on the patient's problem. It raises the following questions: Is this a man who criticizes his girl friend too frequently? Does he ever say anything supportive to her? Does she always bite her tongue and feel resentful when he is critical? Does she have a problem with underassertiveness?

Therapist: Do you just squelch your anger when he does that or does it come out in other ways?

Patient: Oh, it comes out later.

If a therapist is able to define a couple of problems with his patient by the end of the first interview, he has done a lot. The assessment written after the end of the first interview went:

Mrs. Bradley is disheartened for several reasons. First and foremost on her mind are her difficulties with her boy friend Tony, which have caused her to feel lonely and unhappy. Though she is pretty sure things won't work out with him, she still has strong feelings about him. I suspect the last chapter in this relationship hasn't yet been written. She has also been unhappy with her job for a long time. This is adding to her discouragement now.

The present crisis has powerfully lit up memories of her separation with her first husband, by whom she felt utterly rejected without understanding why. Superimposed on all this, I think, is a history of shaky self-esteem caused perhaps by an overly critical stepmother with whom she lived when she was growing up.

In spite of these problems, Mrs. Bradley shows a number of assets which bode well for recovery. She has always worked steadily. She is considered to be highly competent at her job, gets along well with people she works with, and has, at least in the past, enjoyed some parts of her work. She has a couple of friends with whom she talks freely and often. She had an excellent relationship with a therapist whom she saw when she was going through divorce 8 years ago; that experience should make therapy easier now. She has coped reasonably well with stress in the past, though her grief after her divorce lasted longer than usual and I suspect she may have trouble letting go of the present relationship with Tony. She's been in good health, psychologically and physically, has a wide range of interests, and is certainly above average intellectually.

Just before she left the first meeting, I asked her if she had any questions.

Patient: Yes, what should I do?

This is a common question. Several answers are possible.

Therapist: You don't know what to do about Tony and your feelings about him?

About half the time this kind of paraphrase will show the patient's question is more rhetorical than demanding. The discussion will then go on a moment longer. Another response is:

Therapist: I think I need to know more before I can offer advice very freely.

Another possibility is to capitalize on the patient's questions to get the work of therapy started:

Therapist: I don't know yet, but I have some thoughts about how we might approach it together. You could collect some information between now and next week. I'd like to know how often Tony criticizes you every day. Then I'd like to learn how often you keep quiet and how often you retort, and what the consequences are when you do.

Patient: I don't get the second part.

Therapist: Count the number of times each day you stand up for yourself and observe what happens when you do.

The purpose of the therapist's request is to get therapy moving. The task may not be the right one; it can always be changed. It had occurred to me, of course, that the patient might be underassertive. Did she bottle up her anger to the point where small incidents set it off and she would explode? It seemed to me that Mrs. Bradley was in possession of important information: she knew what was not working with Tony. Were there other ways which might work better?

When she returned next week, she told me about several episodes in which she was more assertive. As often happens, she had applied what she had learned to other areas of her life. She said she was tired of taking office work home. She told her boss she would no longer do it and had stuck to her decision. Also, she had her car repaired. A noise she had asked the repairman to fix was still present after she took the car home. She took the car back to be fixed the next day instead of procrastinating, as she usually did.

Her main problem, however, was still her boy friend. Her assertiveness with him had not been as successful. She said that he criticized her three or four times whenever they were together. When she told him how she would like him to change — to be less critical, and more supportive — he accused her of nagging and said he had no intention of changing. She had talked to a girl friend during the week, who gave Mrs. Bradley reason to suspect that Tony was seeing another woman, making the situation more complicated. Her relationship with Tony did not sound promising, but a therapist has to remain cautious when the information is obtained from only one partner.

In the third session, Mrs. Bradley said more about her dissatisfaction with Tony. He had flirted with one of her friends at dinner. He had accepted credit for something she in fact had done. She had answered the phone several times at his house and a woman had asked for him. She felt that he was insensitive to her, never wanted to talk about feelings, was critical of her, and could not be trusted.

Nevertheless, it was hard to let go, she said. He could be witty and perceptive. He could fix anything, and was always willing to help. At the moment he was reroofing her house. He was confident and attractive, and was a good lover.

He had been married twice before, and both wives left him, she surmised, for reasons similar to those she now knew so well.

At the end of the third session, she said:

Patient: Have you known people like us before? Does it ever work out?

Therapist: I only know one side of the story, yours. It's possible, but you've both got some strikes against you as a couple.

Patient: Like what?

Therapist: Like the things you've told me. For one thing, his pattern seems well established. He's been married twice before and you're pretty sure that many of the problems that he's had with his wives are the problems you're facing now. For another, he's told you he doesn't want to change. Instead, he wants you to.

Patient: Would it be worthwhile asking him to come see you too?

Therapist: You want things to work out, don't you?

Patient: (beginning to cry) Yes.

Therapist: I'd be happy to see you together. Do you want to ask him, and then let me know?

He refused, and she decided to break up with him. At this point, the focus of therapy became her loneliness and sadness. People recently separated have a lot to think and cry about. They miss the other person, feel anger and sadness about what has happened and wonder what they might have done differently. When separation occurs, the therapist is most helpful to the patient by listening, by understanding, and by offering reasonable suggestions.

At our sixth meeting, Mrs. Bradley told me that she had seen Tony since our last appointment. She had been excited at first, but had then felt discouraged when she realized the same problems were still there between them.

It may take people a long time to work things out for themselves. A therapist should remember this, and not be impatient if a person fails to make major changes and decisions after a few sessions. People often have to try different things and often repeat their mistakes before they make decisions they can stick with.

With about 10 minutes to go before the end of the fourth session, Mrs. Bradley said:

Patient: Can we talk about something else?

Therapist: Of course.

Patient: I'm going on vacation in August and September. I plan to visit my stepmother for two weeks in Indiana. She still gives me a lot of trouble. I can feel myself getting anxious as I talk about her. Before I go I'd like to talk about what will happen.

Therapist: Fine. Shall we set most of next week's meeting aside to do that?

Patient: Yes.

Several times in the past years, Mrs. Bradley had written her stepmother, asking if she could come visit. Her stepmother had always turned her down. Last Christmas she decided to go anyway and had met with an exceedingly chilly reception. She already knew that her stepmother had rejected her, but there was a family matter which needed attention: 5 years before, when her father had died, it was discovered that he had neglected to make a will. The estate was still tied up and Mrs. Bradley wanted some of the family furniture.

Therapist: Has your sister been able to talk to your mother about it?

Patient: No.

Therapist: Has anyone?

Patient: Not that I know of.

Therapist: It doesn't look very hopeful, I guess.

Patient: No.

Therapist: When you get to Indiana, what will you say when you call her?

A discussion about the ways to approach her mother followed.

Patient: I don't know.

Therapist: Have you thought of going to a lawyer?

Patient: Yes, but I'd like to avoid that hassle if I can. I'll talk to my sister about it.

When she returned from her vacation, she said that she and her sister were forced to go to a lawyer for help. She also said that Tony had sent her flowers twice when she was away. They had begun seeing each other, but with no better luck than before. She complained of another troublesome pattern: whenever they argued, he left. It was impossible to resolve anything with him. She planned to tell him at dinner that night that it was silly for them to continue. At the end of the hour, as she was getting up to leave, she said, "Can I call you when I need another appointment rather than make one now? I think I'm all right. I don't enjoy everything I do, but at least I'm keeping busy." I said yes, that was fine. Five weeks later she called and asked if she could bring her boy friend to our next appointment.

Whenever the therapist has seen one of the partners several times alone, it is wise to spend at least a few minutes alone with the other person before embarking on therapy. By doing this, the therapist learns a bit about the partner; it also gives the partner a chance to look the therapist over. For example:

Therapist: (to Tony) I always like to spend a little time with the person I haven't yet been seeing. Has Diane told you something about our meetings?

What do you see as the problems you and Diane are having? She's told me something, of course, but I'd like to hear your side of it too.

When that is done, the therapist invites the other partner to come in; then he starts over with both of them. He wants the couple to define their problems in each other's presence. After listening to each partner, and after summarizing what he has heard, the therapist can turn to one of them and say, "What would you like your partner to do or change in order to make your life together better?" Then he might ask, "And now for a somewhat harder question. What would you like — or at least be willing — to change about yourself that would make things go better?" He then asks the same questions of the other partner.

The therapist should press for specific examples and find out exactly what the patient means. For example:

Therapist: How would you like Diane to change so that things would go better?

Patient: I'd like her to be more understanding.

Therapist: And that means. . . ?

Patient: Well, to be more affectionate.

Therapist: In what ways?

Patient: I wish she'd come up and spontaneously put her arms around me sometimes.

Therapist: Your example helps me to understand better what you mean by affectionate. What other ways would she act if she were more affectionate?

The therapist should also let the couple know that what goes well between them is as valuable to therapy as what goes badly. This is important; by the time most couples arrive at the therapist's office, they no longer pay attention to what works well in the relationship. They have usually forgotten how to reinforce, compliment, or support each other.

In the first session, the therapist should at least cover the first step and ask each partner to define the problems as he and she sees them. If there is time, the therapist can then go on to the second step by asking each of them what they would like their partner to change and what they themselves would be willing to change. One usually gets through only the first step or part way into the second step before time runs out in the first interview, however. In that case, I give the second step as an assignment between sessions:

Therapist: Would both of you be willing to collect some information between now and our next meeting? First, what changes would you like your partner to make that would make the relationship go more smoothly? And second, what would you be willing to change about yourself so that your relationship would be more satisfactory? You can list as many or as few things as you wish, but please be as specific as you can.

If I do not feel as if I'm giving them too much to do, I might also say:

Therapist: One other thing. I'd like each one of you to make note of something the other person does that you especially like. It doesn't have to be earthshaking, just something the other person does that pleases you, like opening a door, a smile over breakfast, a compliment over dinner — anything you consider thoughtful. I'm interested in what you like about each other, too.

And if I feel that this is too much, I save it for the second or third session.

When Diane and Tony came in together, I saw Tony alone for 15 minutes, then I asked Diane to join us.

Therapist: (turning to Tony) Let me ask you again, now that Diane is here, what do you think are the biggest problems between you?

Tony: She's irritable over small things.

Therapist: Is there a recent example?

Tony: Yeah, we were having dinner last week. Some friends came by the booth and started talking. I couldn't remember their names so I didn't introduce Diane to them. After they left, I could see she was furious. I just wanted to run away.

While it is tempting to take this one problem and start work on it immediately — perhaps by asking the couple to brainstorm together how they could handle the situation better in the future, then maybe asking them to role play the situation — the wisest course so early in therapy is to hold tight and hear them both out.

Therapist: Are there other problems.

Tony: I can't think of any right now.

Therapist: All right. I'll ask Diane the same question. But if other problems come to mind while you're listening, do bring them up when she's through.

The therapist should not allow one partner to interrupt the other too much at the beginning. If one or the other does interrupt, and it looks as if they are simply repeating the same tired patterns, the therapist should take careful note and add,

Therapist: (turning to the interrupting party) I want to hear about what you have to say, but not right now. I want you both to have equal time.

Diane defined three problems. She said that there were cultural differences between them. Tony had grown up in an Italian family in which his father was the undisputed head of the household and was expected to make the major decisions. Women, in turn, were expected to carry out the instructions. Second, she feared that she would be dumped if anyone or anything more important came up in Tony's life. When Tony's children came to visit during the summer, for example, she was rarely invited over. He only called her, it seemed to her, when he did not have anything else to do. Third, she thought they had a problem with communication.

Therapist: Which means?

Patient: We just don't talk enough, especially when feelings are involved. I don't think he talks easily about his feelings.

After summarizing what she had told me, I turned to Tony and asked him what he wanted Diane to change. Only one thing, he said: "I'd like her to be less excitable, less angry, in a whole lot of situations."

She, in turn, said that she would like him to change in several ways: "I'd like him to treat me as a competent person. I work with budgets all the time but he doesn't think I know anything about money. I'd like him to ask me about our budgeting, for example. I'd like him to stick up for himself around his family and for me when I'm around them."

In the first meeting, Diane brought out more problems and saw more ways Tony could change than Tony did. She was clearly more unhappy with the relationship than he. It also seemed to me that she had more invested in the relationship. There were also important stylistic differences between them. Tony was less verbal than Diane. He spoke more slowly and deliberately. Diane looked impatient and fidgety when Tony talked for a long time.

In answer to how he would be willing to change himself, Tony said he wanted to be able to express more feelings. Diane said she would like to be less angry and not view all situations according to whether she felt inferior or superior. In the restaurant, for instance, she felt inferior when Tony did not introduce her. She said she would like to share some of the hurt — which showed as anger — when those situations arose.

As the session neared its end, I asked the couple to collect some information before the next meeting. I asked Tony to keep track, on a 3 X 5 card, of the times during the day he stayed silent when something was bothering him. He was also asked to keep track of the times every day that he talked to Diane about what was on his mind. I did not ask him to change anything. I wanted to find out how often he held things back and how often he shared his feelings with Diane.

I asked Diane to keep track of the times she was sharp with Tony and also the times she felt like being sharp but was instead gentler. As the hour ended, we agreed to meet a week later.

They returned with the information. Tony had withdrawn once, shared his feelings once. Diane had tried to be more gentle half the times she felt annoyed. That took about 4 minutes. They had more pressing things on their minds and wanted to talk about them.

Tony's children lived with their mother in Iowa. When they visited in the summer, Diane felt left out, as she had already told me. She wondered why he did this to her. Tony said he did not think their relationship was stable enough to expose his children more often to Diane. He also told her that the children might come to live with him soon. She was surprised and annoyed that none of this had been said before. This served to identify a frequent problem between them, however: Tony often announced his plans to Diane instead of consulting her first; therefore, she felt left out.

She also said, in front of Tony, that she worried he would leave if she expressed strong feelings about anything. She hated his habit of walking out whenever she would try to talk about her annoyance, irritation, anger, or sadness.

Since the theme of being left out, or being left, pervaded so much of their interaction, it seemed reasonable to talk about it.

Therapist: Diane, could Tony behave differently so you wouldn't feel so left out?

Diane: Well, when he makes decisions which involve both of us, I wish he'd include me.

Therapist: Decisions about?

Diane: Where we go to dinner, when we go out, what we do when the kids are here — things like that.

Therapist: (to Tony) Is this something that makes sense to work on?

Tony: Yeah, I guess so.

Therapist: I've heard you be more enthusiastic.

Tony: It doesn't bother me too much, but if it does Diane, I'm willing to work on it.

Therapist: Is there anything you'd rather work on?

Tony: No.

Sometimes a therapist may have the feeling that the patient's heart is not in therapy. When this happens, there are several approaches. One is to ask the less interested person if he would prefer to work on something else, as I did. Another is for the therapist to check out his or her feelings with the patient. For instance:

Therapist: I get the feeling sometimes that your heart's not quite in this, that you're skeptical about whether therapy, or perhaps things between you and Diane, will work.

A third route is to simply press on, ignore the reluctance for the moment, and bring it up if it becomes obvious again. That is what I chose to do in this instance.

At the end of the hour, I asked Tony to take note of the times he did not consult Diane when a decision was made and, also, the times that he did consult her. I asked Diane to keep track of the times she was consulted.

The following week he came in with a record of four examples of times he consulted her. She had counted two. Why the discrepancy, I asked? As I listened, it became apparent that on one occasion Tony had indeed included Diane while making his decision but she had forgotten about it. The second example was more problematic. The important point, however, was that Diane felt better now that she was being consulted.

Therapist: Have you let him know this during the week, Diane?

Diane: Yes.

Therapist: How?

We continued to pay attention in our sessions to whether Diane was included in Tony's decisions. In the fifth session, Tony said that Diane could still be irritable but not nearly so often. She was happy that he was making an effort to change.

These changes lasted for a month, until his children came to visit. He gradually began to leave her out of his decisions and said he wanted to spend more time with his children. She was afraid to tell him she felt left out for fear he would accuse her of nagging. When she finally got up her nerve and told him she felt left out, he exploded and said he did not see any future in their relationship. She agreed. When I saw her alone a month after the children left, she and Tony had not seen each other for 3 weeks. She seemed more relieved than grief stricken. She said, "I finally realized I couldn't live that on-again, off-again life any more."

She still had things to talk about, however. Her job was bothering her; she felt she was not going anywhere; she was looking for other kinds of work. A useful way to help people with their choices is to listen carefully to see if there are drifts to the conversation which indicate preferences. The therapist can reflect these drifts back to the patient. This may serve to clarify the patient's thoughts and feelings.

Therapist: You've told me about three possibilities. If there's one thing that comes through loud and clear, it's that you don't want to stay in your present job. From the tone of your voice, and from the way you've talked about the other jobs, I get the impression that you're most enthusiastic about the counseling job.

Patient: I think I am too.

Therapist: Well, if you want the job [which she had applied for] what comes next? Do you call them or do they call you?

Patient: They'll call me for an interview.

Therapist: Any problem with that?

Patient: Yes! Those kinds of interviews make me so nervous. I've never been able to handle them.

Therapist: I could help you with that if you want. Once your interview has been scheduled, why don't you call me and we'll talk about it.

Patient: That sounds good.

Therapist: A good way to prepare for this would be to find out what a committee like this is likely to ask you. Do you know anyone who could tell you?

Patient: Yes.

Two weeks later she phoned for an appointment. She had learned that she would undoubtedly be asked by someone what she would do if a black student and a white student got in a fight. The interviewer would want to know how she would resolve it and what her views on discipline were. I played the part of a tough-minded black man on the committee who challenged her on not only discipline but also what she would do if she found marijuana on one of the students during school. After three or four trials, I said:

Therapist: You sound pretty good. You seem poised, prepared, thoughtful. There's one observation which might be useful to you, however: If you find yourself stuck for an immediate answer, there's nothing wrong with saying, 'Let me think about that for a minute,' and perhaps even asking a few questions while you're thinking about the answer.

Three weeks later, the patient got her job as a counselor. The interview had gone well; in fact it had been easier than she anticipated.

She consulted me again 8 months later. She had just been told by her gynecologist that she needed a hysterectomy because of fibroid tumors, and was worried about how surgery would affect her psychologically. She thought that she might have the same feelings of panic and internal turmoil, especially self-doubt, that had followed her divorce 8 years before. She also said that she was nervous at work. When she was faced with a relatively minor task at work, she began to worry that she would make a mistake. When I asked her more closely what she was worried about, she admitted that she feared she would lose her job, even her mind, and end up in a hospital for the rest of her life. At the same time that she was imagining these catastrophes, she said she felt apprehension, depression, and, also, burning sensations in her chest.

Therapist: You're worried you'll end up as a basket case, that you'll be hospitalized the rest of your life. Is that the worst of it?

Patient: No. I'm afraid no one will be there to support me if I have a breakdown.

Again, the theme of being left alone appeared.

Therapist: (nodding first; then, after a minute, softly): You said you have friends. Do you call them when you feel bad?

Patient: No.

Therapist: Because?

Patient: I don't want to be a burden.

Therapist: You've mentioned several times that people have called you when they need to talk. Are they a burden?

Patient: Sometimes — but usually not.

Therapist: Why are you different from them?

It was here that I began to wonder again about something that had come up in one of our first meetings: her underassertiveness. People with low self-esteem often feel they do not have the right to ask for help from others when they feel troubled.

Therapist: You said you have trouble asking for help, but I wonder if it's part of a bigger problem. Do you have trouble expressing your feelings and needs?

Patient: I'm sure I do. I have trouble standing up for myself.

Therapist: Any recent examples?

Patient: Yes.

Her roommate, who did not share the cooking and housekeeping as she had promised to do before she moved in, was calling her "controlling" whenever she brought up the topic of sharing. A house painter, for a second example, had splattered paint on her windows. When she complained, he had told her that she worried too much. She felt pushed around.

Therapist: You've said a lot in the last few minutes. You feel you'll be abandoned if things go bad. You also feel that people are pushing you around. Which of these things would you like to work on first?

Patient: I'd like to talk about my roommate.

Therapist: Okay. Give me an idea of what your roommate says to you that puts you in a bind.

Patient: Whenever I bring up something I think she should do, she calls me 'controlling.'

Therapist: What happens then?

Patient: I don't know what to do! I feel guilty.

Therapist: Then she doesn't do the job either?

Patient: Exactly.

Therapist: Why don't we think of a different way to handle it? Let me play you and you be her.

Patient: Okay.

Therapist: (role-playing Diane) Sue, this is hard to bring up, but we've got to talk again about the dishes and the laundry.

Patient: (role-playing her roommate) What about the dishes?

Therapist: It bothers me when they sit around dirty in the sink for a couple days.

Patient: Why?

Therapist: I can't answer that. All I can say is that they do and I'd like to come to some agreement about them.

Patient: Oh, Diane, you're so controlling.

Therapist: Perhaps. But what are we going to do about the dishes?

I pointed out to Mrs. Bradley why she had trouble talking to her roommate: the roommate sidetracked issues by accusing Mrs. Bradley of having a problem whenever Mrs. Bradley brought an issue up.

Therapist: Notice that I ignored those remarks and just stuck to the point. Can you do the same thing?

Patient: I think so.

Therapist: All right. Why don't we reverse roles. You be yourself and I'll be Susan.

I rehearsed the sequence with Mrs. Bradley several times until she had it well in mind. I encouraged her to rehearse the troublesome sequence before she confronted her roommate. I also encouraged her to stick to the point and not be thrown off by her roommate's guilt-provoking labels. People often receive the kind of behavior they are willing to tolerate from others. In many instances, patients have to set firm limits and demand change from those close to them before their own situation will improve.

When she returned a week later, she said that she had worked out an arrangement with her roommate. She also told the painter exactly what she wanted and he had agreed to it.

Therapist: What accounts for the change?

Patient: Well, it was good to come last week and talk things out. I got some ideas. After I'd left, I decided to do what I had to do instead of putting it off.

A year later she remained reasonably satisfied with her work. She had not yet found a steady boy friend, but she had been dating different men. She called me several times after that last meeting, once to ask for a gynecologic referral, another time to tell me she was thinking seriously of joining a group; she wanted my advice.

Many cases require the therapist be able to use different therapeutic approaches to different problems. In this case, I did couples therapy, helped the woman manage a mild grief reaction, aided her in dealing with an uncooperative stepmother, role played a job interview, and encouraged her to be more assertive when she dealt with her roommate.

I respected her position with her boy friend and did not push her to make a decision about him before she was ready. I asked her in every instance for specific examples of the problems she told me about. She was always able to provide them, and that made the work of therapy relatively easy.

A Proposition

Most of the problems that a therapist and patient work on in the course of therapy are problems that the patient has brought to the meeting; they arose before the patient and the therapist ever met. New and unexpected problems may arise, however, in the course of treatment. In the case that follows, an expected and troubling problem developed between a male therapist and a female patient. The principles of management would obviously be similar if the therapist had been a woman and the patient a man.

A 27-year-old male dental student consulted me because of marital problems. He and his wife came to see me together. Six weeks before, he said, he had announced to his wife that he no longer loved her. He had felt that way for several months. He had two complaints about her. She was too dependent on him. She had trouble making decisions without him and did not have much of a life of her own. Nor did he feel that he could talk to her about important issues. If he brought up money, for example, she would say archly, "Well, why don't you manage it better?" Instead of consultation, he would receive criticism. He believed that he would be better off alone but had not moved out because he did not yet want to break up his family, which included a 6-year-old daughter.

His wife took a much different stand. She said she had always loved her husband and wanted to stay married. She was shocked when her husband told her he did not love her.

They had both grown up in professional families. Her father had been very indulgent with her. He had died of cancer, a year before, at age 55. She was both angry and sad following his death. She said, "I kept thinking, how could he do this to me?" He had bailed her out of numerous jams, especially as she had lurched through adolescence using drugs indiscriminately, falling into promiscuity for a short time, running away from home twice, and even once making a suicide attempt. She described her mother as a cold, unemotional, alcoholic woman who had no close friends.

During the interview, her husband seemed much more relaxed than she, less driven, certainly less frantic. I wondered if there was a significant tempo problem between them. One partner who thinks, speaks, and moves much more quickly or slowly than his or her partner can bother the other partner exceedingly.

Toward the end of the first meeting, I decided to talk to each of them alone for a few minutes.

Therapist: (to husband) How do you think I can best help you?

Husband: I don't know if you can. I've lost my feelings for her. I thought you could make life more livable for us for a while.

He told me that his wife had been in therapy several years before with an elderly therapist who had since retired. The husband also said that if he decided to move out, he wanted to leave his wife in someone's hands. His present living arrangements with her were only temporary, he admitted. In another year, when his wife finished her training to be a court stenographer, he would leave her regardless.

I was faced immediately with a question: Should I undertake a course of treatment with this couple, even though I felt the marriage was probably doomed, if only to help the couple make things easier for themselves temporarily? It seemed that the husband had given up on the marriage, and it is usually a fatal sign when a person says he has lost his feeling for his spouse. I thought they deserved a try at therapy. After all, situations are not always as hopeless as they first seem, and besides, was there anything to lose?

Therapy was tough. The husband said that he was satisfied with himself but that, for the sake of time together, he would be willing to make any changes that might improve the marriage for his wife. In response to his wife's criticism, he agreed to try to be more talkative at dinner time (to ask her about her day, for example), to be less argumentative, and to compliment her occasionally.

She also said that there was very little she wanted to change about herself, but she agreed, for example, not to nag her husband if he came home late from work in the evening.

The couple returned for a second meeting. The husband had tried to compliment his wife about something – the meals she prepared, the loving ways she talked with their daughter – several times a day. His wife had tried not to nag him, but it was hard. She said, "When I feel critical, like when he's staying away, what am I supposed to do?"

The staggering news of the week was that the husband had told his wife that he was involved with another woman and intended soon to move out and stay with her. The marriage was over. There was no reason for them to continue seeing me as a couple, he said. The wife, however, said that she wanted to continue therapy as a couple. She needed support, she said, and also wanted to keep talking to her husband. She hoped the marriage could somehow last. Her husband said that as long as he lived with her he would call her if he stayed out past 11:00 at night. She told him that was the least he could do.

His wife came alone for the next visit. Although her husband had called her as he had promised to do, he rarely came home. She could not stand it any more and told him to get out; he left.

The tone of therapy shifted markedly. What had started off as a request for marital therapy changed into the management of a grief reaction. The first principle in helping a person with a grief reaction is not to block it. The therapist should not dampen the patient's feelings with premature reassurance. The therapist should listen carefully to what happened to the patient, and try to understand why it occurred. Anger and sadness are usually comingled with rage, despair, blame, and regret, especially if one has been left.

The therapist should not be thrown off by the patient's unrealistic demands for, say, medication or for frequent appointments. People in crisis act differently than they do when their lives are stable. A therapist who is level-headed and reasonable has a steadying effect on an unstable person. A therapist should also be prepared to support any reasonable plans the patient is able to make. I do not hesitate to tell patients that grief does not last forever, but that discouragement is common for weeks and even months after a loss. I occasionally reassure patients that they can take steps to help themselves get along better with other people in the future, as I did, for example, in this case:

Therapist: Why do you think he left?

Patient: My temper.

Therapist: I know anger can be a real problem between two people.

Patient: I just know that if I hadn't exploded and thrown things at him, we'd be together now.

Therapist: (nods).

Patient: (despairingly) But what can I do now to control it?

Therapist: There are several things you can do.

The therapist should be empathic and sympathetic with the patient only if those feelings are honestly there. Statements like, "I know what you mean," can be helpful if heartfelt, but I think that understanding is best shown by careful listening, accurate paraphrases, and nonverbal responses — a look of genuine sympathy, for example.

The therapist should make himself more than usually available, either by planning more frequent visits or by arranging for phone calls between sessions. Occasionally medications are called for. Sleeplessness by itself can be particularly demoralizing, and a good night's sleep can do wonders for a person.

A person in crisis will sometimes ask, "How can I best cope with the way I'm feeling now?" Sometimes this question is rhetorical. But when it is not, I may suggest that the patient talk to friends and solicit their support during the crisis. I also encourage patients in crisis to stick to their regular habits if they can, since crises throw us off our routines, which in turn adds to stress and makes the task of coping with problems more difficult.

Therapist: I know this may sound obvious, but it's important to eat three good meals a day, to continue to work if you can, to drink only moderately, and to try to get eight hours of sleep.

At our next meeting, the fourth, the woman started the session by asking: "Do I need help?" It may be a patient's way of asking if she's doing the right thing. It may also be a request for reassurance. In this case, however, I worried about the question. I had come to know her well enough to know that if I said yes, she would have said something like, "Well, you're the one who thinks I need help. Help me." There are several responses to the question "Do I need help?" In this instance, I said, "What do you think?" At other times, I have asked, "What brings that question up?"

In our 5th interview, 3 weeks after her husband had left, she began with, "How was your week?" I said, "It was fine, thanks. More to the point, how was yours?" But later in the interview this conversation occurred:

Patient: I don't know much about you.

Therapist: What would you like to know?

Patient: Are you married?

Therapist: Yes.

Patient: Do you have any children?

Therapist: Yes, three.

I wondered why the patient was asking me these questions. Patients have a right to ask any questions they wish, and I believe they have a right to know something about the therapist. But at the same time, the therapist should be alert to issues which may be behind a patient's personal questions.

In this case, the questions disguised one of the most difficult problems that can emerge in the course of therapy: a patient's romantic feelings toward a therapist. Romantic feelings are often concealed at first. The therapist's index of suspicion should be high when a patient asks repeatedly for personal information, complains that the therapist does not take enough time, phones frequently for advice, asks to be called by her first name or calls the therapist by his, tells the therapist that her sex life picks up after their sessions, or dresses better as therapy proceeds.

The therapist's reactions to the patient during the session may be a cue to the presence of romantic feelings. If the therapist notices that it is hard to listen to what the patient is saying because he is distracted by how the patient looks, talks, or moves, if he entertains sexual fantasies about the patient during or after the session, or if he finds himself unexplainably tense and defensive, he should be alert to the possibility of erotic feelings.

Once I suspect that a patient may have romantic feelings toward me, I ask about the feelings with a question such as:

Therapist: Sometimes people have strong feelings of different kinds about their therapist. I wonder if you've had some feelings about me?

In this case, the whole issue came to light when, toward the end of one of our later sessions she said:

Patient: Would you like to come over Friday night?

Therapist: No.

Patient: Why?

Therapist: For a number of reasons.

Patient: Like what?

Therapist: Well, you came to me for help because things were going badly in your life. If I were to accept your invitation I would feel as if I were exploiting you, for one thing.

Patient: God, exploit me!

Therapist: I can't do that.

Patient: Look, I'm not suggesting we do anything. All I asked was whether you'd like to come over Friday night.

Therapist: In order to . . . ?

Patient: Talk, just like we do here. I consider you a friend. I don't do anything different in here than I do when I'm talking with a friend.

Therapist: I view it differently. Friendship may be part of our relationship, but that's not all there is to it. It would be hard for me to give you the kind of help I think you need if I were involved with you outside of therapy.

An exchange like this is not meant to stop a patient in her tracks. Instead, it is meant to set limits on what the therapist will and will not do. The patient should not feel punished for expressing her feelings or offering an invitation, but I believe she should know where the therapist stands.

Setting the limits to the relationship is only the first step in dealing with these powerful feelings. The therapist must also try to understand why they have occurred. It seemed that this woman had a dependent, overindulgent relationship with her father, whom she idealized. She had married young, and had probably expected her husband to act toward her much as her father had. She had not learned to work as a partner in the marriage but only as a person who was continually disappointed that her husband did not wish to fill her father's role. It was hardly a surprise that she was thrown into turmoil when her husband left, and it was also no surprise she became emotionally involved with a male therapist, a doctor, who was viewed as older, stable, dependable, and caring — much like her father. Also a person who has few attachments may overinvest emotionally in those few existing attachments.

Recognition of the problem, limit-setting, and an understanding of why these feelings have occurred are all critical for proper management. Sometimes the therapist must explain to the patient why it would be unwise to alter their relationship; sometimes a patient's misconceptions have to be corrected.

Patient: I don't know why you can't loosen up and have a drink with me. Do you wonder what other people will think?

Therapist: There are many reasons. That's one.

Patient: I'm surprised. I thought you were the kind of person who was more independent of what other people thought of you.

Therapist: Not at all. I care a great deal about what people think of me, especially my colleagues.

Another approach I use is to ask patients what their fantasies about me are. Then, also in fantasy, I have them imagine possible consequences of their fantasies. For example:

Therapist: In your fantasy, where do we go? What do we do together?

Patient: Maybe we'd go on a picnic somewhere.

Therapist: Where?

Patient: Maybe Columbia Park.

Therapist; Would we do anything else while we're there?

Patient: Go through the museum.

Therapist: Okay. Suppose we did that. And suppose we've eaten our lunch and we're just getting ready to leave the museum and somebody we both know walks in. And let's suppose, further, that he's been having some troubles with his wife and has thought of coming in to see me with her. What will he think? Where will he turn then?

This particular sequence illustrates what behavior therapists call "covert sensitization," that is, helping a person become more aware of the consequences of an action by imagining the consequences in fantasy.[1] With my patient, the conversation went like this:

Patient: I'd like to get together and have a couple of glasses of wine at, say, the Dandelion Pub.

Therapist: And then?

Patient: I don't know — dinner, maybe back at my place.

Therapist: Suppose we do that. Then suppose we go another time and then suppose you don't hear from me for a week. What would happen then?

Patient: I'd probably call you.

Therapist: And suppose I said I was busy.

Patient: I'd try again.

Therapist: And if I was busy again?

Patient: I don't know.

Therapist: And what would you have then? By that time, of course, therapy with us would be long over. You wouldn't have me as a therapist or as a friend. How would you feel?"

Patient: Probably pissed.

Therapist: Exactly, and I wouldn't blame you. Wouldn't you feel kind of exploited?

Patient: Yeah.

Therapist: I can't see why I'd want to do that to you.

This kind of conversation has risks — one does not want to lead on the patient or make her feel as if she has been led into a trap — but it can be done successfully if the therapist is tactful and kind. Behind the propositions that patients sometimes make to their therapists are needs for companionship, for relief of loneliness, for status, for self-esteem. It would be callow to think of these only as manipulations on the patient's part. Patients who proposition their therapists put themselves out on a limb and here, as elsewhere in therapy, Frieda Fromm-Reichmann's first principle of therapy still holds: first of all, do nothing to harm a person's self-respect.[2]

Interpretative remarks by the therapist, aimed at clarifying handicapping patterns of overinvolvement with men or aimed at bringing out the connection between a woman's past history with her father and her current feelings toward the therapist are not very helpful when romantic feelings are at their height. In fact, when feelings are so intense, an interpretation may sound more like punishment than a helpful remark. It is better to hold off interpreting until the peak of feeling and emotion has passed. Interpretations are best made when there is evidence that the connection between past and present events is already close to the patient's awareness, as shown through dreams, slips and errors in speech, etc.[3] There is a place for interpretation in the management of romantic feelings, but the therapist must possess a good sense of timing.

When therapists are faced with strong romantic feelings, they should not withdraw and become cool and distant with their patient. Therapists tend to pull away in their haste not to flirt or not to lead the patient on. Unfortunately, this can look like rejection. If the patient feels this, his or her chance of learning anything from therapy is poor.

Many, though not all, of the cases which are complicated by erotic feelings end successfully, in that the patient learns something and the termination of therapy is mutual. If, after several months, it is clear that there is no progress in therapy, or if the romantic feelings take a more ominous turn — towards a delusion, for example — it is best to refer the patient to another therapist. I once treated a 50-year-old woman, the wife of a businessman, for a year and a half. She had never developed a very meaningful life of her own and was unhappy with her marriage. Toward what turned out to be the end of our therapy, I finally realized she had strong romantic feelings about me. We talked about them, and they seemed to be under control. Two weeks later, however, she formed the unshakeable belief that she and I were going to catch a plane to Bermuda together, that we were going to get married, and presumably, live happily ever after. Even after a brief hospitalization, medication, and a course of conjoint therapy with her husband, the delusions returned and I referred her to a female therapist her own age.

Psychoanalysts from Freud on have appreciated the great difficulty presented by patients who develop a romantic transference to their therapist in the course of treatment.[4-6] No doubt therapy has foundered because of intense romantic feelings in a good many cases, but a colleague and I have recently discovered that as many as two-thirds of women who develop strong romantic and sexual feelings toward their therapists remain in therapy (though the therapy was not psychoanalysis) and work through their feelings.[7]

There are of course many ways in which a therapist is like a good friend, or, for that matter like a good father, mother, coach, or teacher. But three characteristics of the therapist's role distinguish it from the others.[8] First, reciprocity and mutuality are limited. The focus of therapy is the patient, not the therapist. The therapist puts the patient first, which means that the patient does most of the talking. The therapist does not usually attempt to share his personal life with the patient, though he may wish to share parts of it on occasion.

Second, the time, the place, and the topics are limited. The necessary limitation of time and place are obvious. Clearly, all topics which come into the patient's mind cannot be discussed. The content of therapy sessions usually centers on the patient's current problems.

Third, there is an initial commitment to termination. A therapeutic relationship is intended to be transient in most cases. Therapy, after all, should promote the goal not only of self-understanding but also of independence.

These points should be kept in mind because some patients will explicitly or implicitly ask that the therapeutic relationship be turned into a friendship. This means that the patient will want to see the therapist outside the office, call him or her at will, talk matters over at social occasions, etc.

The professional role of a therapist is hard enough without adding other roles to it. Besides, most therapists would not want their patients as friends, for any number of reasons. What should be done, then, when patients nominate the therapist for friendship when the therapist has not nominated them?

Patient: Why can't we just be friends?

Therapist: And by friends you mean?

Patient: Someone you can invite to a party, someone you can phone when you like.

Therapist: I can't do that. Doing therapy properly is hard enough. I couldn't be your therapist and your friend at the same time.

Patient: I'm not asking you to be my therapist, I'd rather have you as a friend.

Therapist: You may have come to the wrong place if that's what you want.

or

Therapist: Perhaps one of our goals in here should be to get you the friends you want, but I can't do it personally. Friendships are chancy. There's no guarantee our relationship would work out as friendship. Where would you go then if you needed help?

The dental student's wife presented several other problems to me before therapy ended. She called me before the 14th session and said that a psychiatrist whom her mother had known had called her and asked her to come in for a visit. This psychiatrist had taken care of several family members in the past and, the patient said, her mother called him because she did not feel her daughter was improving fast enough. The patient had in fact gone ahead and met with the psychiatrist, who had advised her to admit herself to the hospital for treatment, perhaps even for shock therapy. She wanted to know what I thought about this advice.

What should I say? I was at first angry with the psychiatrist for interfering without an invitation. But then, as I thought about the situation, I realized I knew very little about it.

Patient: It was very upsetting. Why did he say what he did? Do you think I need shock?

Therapist: Not that I can see. But there's so much I don't understand. I

think it would be best if I talked to Dr. Sanders to see what he
had in mind. Then you and I could talk about it.

Patient: Fine.

The old rule — when in doubt seek more information — was again up-
held. The psychiatrist told me the patient herself had called him and asked
for an appointment! It clearly would have been a mistake for me to have
called the psychiatrist and accused him of interfering with my patient. The
psychiatrist said that he had recommended a number of possible courses
to the patient; he had mentioned shock treatment only in passing. The
psychiatrist and I agreed to call each other, with the patient's permission,
if other discrepancies came up.

At my next session with the patient, the conversation went like this:

Patient: Did you talk to Dr. Sanders?

Therapist: Yes, I did. He said that you'd called him for an appointment
and that he'd called you back to set it up.

Patient: That's not true.

It would be a futile exercise to argue about who did what. Instead, I
chose to raise another issue:

Therapist: Well, no matter. I couldn't help wondering, though, if you decided to see Dr. Sanders because you weren't happy with the
progress you've made in here.

Patient: That's right.

At that point, she and I had a discussion about the goals of therapy,
her expectations, and her dissatisfactions. The patient said that her goal
was to "get over these feelings," meaning her loneliness, her despair, her
anger, and her resentment toward her husband.

How were her dissatisfactions with therapy to be met? I knew by now
that the patient was having a much harder time coping with her loss than
most separated women I had seen. Furthermore, I could see that she had
refused consistently to make plans that would reduce her vulnerability to
loneliness. She did not make plans for the weekends, for example, when
her feelings of discouragement were most acute. The patient seemed to be
saying, "I want you to take my symptoms away, but I don't want to
change anything about myself."

This is difficult to work with. I realized that her inability to take steps
to help herself more was probably part of an old pattern she had established with her father; whenever she was in trouble, her father had taken

care of her, rescued her; but now he was dead. I chose not to explain this to her, but said instead:

Therapist: You're in a tough spot, I know. You feel lonely and isolated. But I also know, from what you've told me, that at times when you've felt loneliest, you've called people up, gone out, and tried to keep busy. You found out that you felt better when you did those things. Does it make sense to try them again?

She said that it did not, that it was too hard, that she was too depressed. I did not feel she needed hospitalization. The choice is hers now, I thought.

The patient failed to show up for her appointment two sessions later, but she called back several days after that to say that she had forgotten the appointment because she had been so busy at work. She asked if she could reschedule it. After several more visits, however, she declared that she had decided not to come anymore. She was not satisfied with her progress. She had expected to be feeling better by now. I asked her what she might want from another therapist. She said she wanted to set some goals. I said that sounded reasonable and asked what kinds of goals. She said she did not know and would think about them.

When a patient wants to go elsewhere, the therapist should try to understand not only why but also how he or she might have handled the case better. I no longer try to talk patients into staying with me in therapy. Many have already made up their minds to leave before they bring it up with me, anyway. Besides, patients who are unhappy with me may very well be right when they believe they would do better with another therapist. This is not the happiest way to end therapy, of course, but the therapist can at least make it easier for the patient by continuing to show the patience, understanding, and helpfulness which should characterize the therapeutic relationship from the beginning. It is well to remember, also, that unhappy people can make hasty decisions which they afterwards regret. A therapist should leave the door open to people who are clearly in trouble.

In this case, the patient indeed left therapy and sought out another psychiatrist, whom she saw for two visits. A month later she called back and asked if she could start therapy with me again. She was unhappy with the psychiatrist, who she said talked more than she did. I said that I would be willing to see her again, but only if she agreed to look into the possibilities of group therapy in addition to her individual work, if she agreed to limit the number of phone calls she made to me each week (this had become a troublesome issue by the end of therapy), and if she agreed to let me talk with the other psychiatrist. She said she would think about these conditions for a few days and call me back.

She never did. A year later, I called and asked her how she was. She told me that she still had many bad days and that her mood had not improved much. She had threatened to commit suicide on several occasions and had been hospitalized twice during the year, once for a month, the second time for three weeks. She had been given numerous psychotropic drugs, none of which had helped. Her present psychiatrist, an older man, was now thinking about prescribing another type of antidepressant medication.

This was by no means all he was doing, however. In the past 6 months, he had set up an extensive social network for her. Six other people were involved besides himself. The patient had been instructed to call one of these people every day of the week and talk with them for at least 30 minutes. If she did not call, they were to call her. She visited the psychiatrist three times a week for an hour, at 3 dollars a visit. The patient and the members of her network, including the psychiatrist, sometimes had dinner together. Every 2 months the team and the patient would meet together and talk. The woman said she was a little embarrassed to be so dependent on so many people, but she had not had to enter the hospital again since her network had been formed, and she had been able to work every day.

She admitted that she had wanted me to be an intimate friend and not a therapist. My refusal to meet her request had been the main reason she had quit therapy, she said.

I was very impressed by what the psychiatrist and several other people had been willing and able to do for her. They recognized that she was desperately lonely, and without a friend. I suspect that the psychiatrist probably realized that this woman had a borderline personality and knew that neither he nor anyone could alone shoulder the entire burden of her treatment. He was generous enough to see her at a price she could afford and was able to extend himself well beyond the traditional psychiatrist's role. It was also, no doubt, fortuitous that he was 56 years old, just about the same age as her deceased father.

This case illustrates the fact that intense feelings that occur as patient and therapist work together in the course of therapy can permanently disrupt treatment. It illustrates one way to deal with feelings when they arise. It demonstrates the importance of avoiding premature criticism of a colleague and obtaining more information when a confusing situation arises.

It also shows what one therapist can learn from another about the management of a case if the trouble is taken to get a follow-up.

REFERENCES

1. Cautela JR: Covert sensitization. Psychol Rep 20: 459–468, 1967
2. Fromm–Reichmann F: Principles of Intensive Psychotherapy. Chicago, University of Chicago Press, 1950, p 10
3. Offenkrantz W, Tobin A: Psychoanalytic psychotherapy, in Freedman DX, Dyrud JE (eds): American Handbook of Psychiatry (ed 2), vol. 5. New York, Basic Books, 1975, pp 183-205
4. Freud S: Observations on transference-love. vol. 12, London, Hogarth Press, Standard Edition, 1958, pp 158-171
5. Rappaport EA: The management of an erotized transference. Psychoanal 25: 515–529, 1956
6. Blum HP: The concept of Erotized Transference. J Am Psychoanal Assoc 21: 61–92, 1973
7. U'Ren RC, Van Rheenen FJ: Romantic and sexual feelings toward the therapist. Unpublished manuscript, 1979
8. Gilmore S: The Counselor-in-Training. Englewood Cliffs, N.J.: Prentice-Hall, 1973, pp 119-120

A Diagnostic Predicament

In the medical tradition, to diagnose is to determine by examination the nature or identity of a problem. Correct identification should of course suggest proper treatment. Most patients who come to a therapist are easy to diagnose. But occasionally one comes along who is not.

A 60-year-old woman consulted me at the recommendation of a general practitioner. She told me on the telephone that she wanted an appointment. Her husband, 64, had a past history of drinking bouts and depression, and had retired from his job just three months before. He began drinking heavily one afternoon, threatening not only to kill his wife, but also to kill anyone who might come to the house if she called them. His wife was so frightened that she left him for a week, considered staying away permanently, and returned only after she was reassured, by her daughter, that her husband was back to normal and no longer drinking. But she was now beginning to worry that he might start drinking again. She had made up her mind to leave, this time for good, if it happened once more. Could anything be done for him, she asked? There was one other problem: she had no idea of how much money they had. Though she and her husband had been married 40 years, he had never told her how much he earned. If she left, she said, she deserved some of the money. Perhaps, she suggested, her husband might be willing to talk about money in the presence of a third person.

Therapist: It sounds as if there's plenty to talk about. Is your husband willing to come?

Patient: Yes, I think so. He doesn't want me to leave. He's promised not to drink any more. He'll come if I ask him to.

Therapist: I have an appointment available next Monday at 3:00. Would that be good for you?

Patient: Yes.

Therapist: Do you know where my office is?

Patient: Yes, I think so.

Therapist: Good. See you at 3:00.

Before the interview, I sat down and thought about what I knew about older men in general and this man in particular. For a man of this age, what were the likeliest diagnostic possibilities? Depression, dementia, or periodic alcoholism were probably the main considerations, but there were many questions in my mind. Was it retirement that had set him off? Was it something else? Did his past depressions precede or follow the onset of his drinking? Did he, or would he now have, the major symptoms of depression: insomnia, loss of appetite, low mood, inability to concentrate or remember? What was his usual personality like? Had it changed recently? Did he have any history of medical problems? Was there any family history of depression, alcoholism, or dementia?

After introducing myself in the waiting room, I walked down the hall with the couple and thought about the impression they had made on me. It has been said that you see things in the first interview you never see again. The man was a strong, well-built person about 6 feet tall who weighed around 200 pounds. He took care in dressing and seemed very reserved. His face was red and a bit blotchy, but I could not smell alcohol on his breath. His wife was much smaller, about 5 feet, 2 inches, and very pretty. She looked worried rather than depressed and was dressed nicely. I began the interview:

Therapist: You called me last week, Mrs. Casey, and said there were things that were worrying you. Have you and your husband talked about them yet?

Patient: Yes:

Therapist: Well, in our brief conversation last week you mentioned something that had happened three months ago that to you was very upsetting. You also said your husband had never talked about money. Was there anything else?

Mrs. Casey: No.

Therapist: "Okay. Could you start, Mrs. Casey, and tell me what hap-
                pened in July?

Shortly after her husband had retired, he suddenly changed, she said.
He grew silent, remained in his den downstairs, and began to drink. On the
third day after his drinking began, his wife was sitting at the kitchen table,
eating. He quietly entered through a door behind her, looked at her unemo-
tionally, and said, "Enjoy it. That's the last thing you'll ever eat."

Terrified, she left the house and stayed with friends but continued to
call her husband twice a day in order to stay in touch. At her friend's urging, she called the county sheriff, who was reluctant to take action. When
Mrs. Casey told her husband that she had called the police, he said, "No
one's going to get me. I've got guns ready and I'll use them." When she
called home two hours later, he had calmed down but told her he suspected the phone line was bugged.

His drinking had begun in 1941, when he was in the Army. In 1951, he
was unexpectedly assigned overseas. He felt bitter, angry, disappointed,
depressed, and he began drinking heavily then. In 1956 he was discharged
from the Army, his wife told me, with a diagnosis of manic-depressive illness. In 1958, his father (quite against the son's wishes) had him committed to a veterans' hospital in California for drinking, where he remained
for 6 months. When he was discharged, he vowed never to return. Another
drinking episode had occurred 4 years before the present one. It seemed to
come on suddenly and his wife did not think that he had been depressed
beforehand.

His erratic behavior and drinking in July ended abruptly after 8 days.
He had been fine since then. His wife said, "He can be like Dr. Jekyll and
Mr. Hyde."

I also learned in the first interview that he had always been an extremely taciturn, unexpressive, conscientious man. He had an excellent
academic record during the 2 years he had attended college. He had never
enjoyed close friendships and had always been rather unemotional with
other people. He had never been hospitalized for medical reasons. His wife
had not observed any lasting change in his personality. He had none of
the symptoms of depression. His own father had a history of erratic behavior and intermittent drinking.

It was true that he had never talked about money with his wife. Even
after 40 years, he insisted that she pay half of everything they did together.
For a long time he had also been suspicious that his wife had been unfaithful to him. He had always worried that she would run off with his money.

They were separated for 3 years, between 1958 and 1961. His wife took the major responsibility for raising their two children.

He said that, yes, he had drunk too much in the past, especially when life got him down, but that it would not happen again. He denied that he had ever threatened his wife. He also told me that he had no desire to discuss money with his wife. He would never have come to see a therapist on his own, he said, but he did not want his wife to leave him.

His wife impressed me as an intelligent woman who had managed to cope effectively with past crises. She had several close friends whom she relied heavily upon. She looked distraught. Her husband was a different matter. He sat stolidly while his wife talked, his speech lacked spontaneity, his mood was flat and he showed little emotion, but he did not look depressed. He spoke only in response to direct questions. There was a slightly vacuous quality to his talk. Once he got talking, though, he talked at length and tended to repeat himself. Three or four times, for example, he said that his drinking had never interfered with his ability to do his work.

At the end of the first interview, my problem list was:

1. An episode of unpredictable and threatening behavior probably associated with intermittent episodic drinking.
2. Marital difficulties associated with:
   a. Intermittent alcoholism.
   b. His inability to show feelings.
   c. His unwillingness to discuss money and her bitterness about that.

I considered the possibility of manic-depressive illness in this man. I also thought that the diagnosis of a brain syndrome, perhaps an early dementia, should be ruled out: Here was a 60-year-old man who showed a flat and empty countenance and who had recovered from a rather worrisome episode in the summer. I also entertained the possibility of a frontal lobe tumor or a small stroke.

My plan was as follows:

1. I need more information about him.
   a. I want to know whether or not he has evidence of an organic brain syndrome. I will do a mental status examination next visit. Psychological testing will be considered, as will a neurologic work-up.
   b. I would like to ask his permission to send away for records of his first hospitalization in 1956.
   c. I would like to know more about his medical history.

2. There is evidence that lithium carbonate is helpful when intermittent drinking is associated with depression. If I get the proper evidence, I may propose this treatment to him.
3. I set up another appointment in 2 days.

In the second interview, I learned that the patient did not give a history of clear-cut mood swings to support the diagnosis of manic-depressive illness. His urge to drink usually came upon him when he was simply upset by something or other, but this seemed no reason to conclude that his drinking was a result of depression.

His mental status examination was perfectly normal. His memory was excellent; he was oriented to person, place, and time; his fund of information was excellent; and he performed calculations effortlessly. On this second meeting I noticed that he seemed more talkative, less reticent, and more spontaneous than he had been two days before. His wife said that there was nothing peculiar about his behavior now. But she was still afraid of him because of his behavior 3 months before.

His physical examination was also normal, with the exception of his blood pressure, which was slightly elevated at 130/94, taken in his right arm while he was sitting. He was willing to take the usual examinations that supplement the physical examination — blood count, urinalysis, chest x-ray, serology, electrocardiogram (all of which were also normal) — but he refused me permission to write to the verterans' hospital to obtain his past psychiatric records. "I don't think there'd be any need for that," he said.

A third appointment was set up. I wanted to tell the Caseys what my impressions were. I also wanted to tell them about lithium and to ask them if they would recognize, either of them, what warning signs Mr. Casey might show if he became depressed and started drinking again.

Every case creates its own atmosphere and makes its own demands. Mrs. Casey's initial request on the telephone had sounded reasonable to me. Was there anything to be done about her husband's condition? But, first, what *was* the condition? All I could say for sure was that her husband was an intermittently heavy drinker. His drinking episodes were usually but not always brought on by worries in his life. Were these episodes symptomatic of periodic depressions? And in spite of the patient's somewhat empty exterior, there was no evidence he had brain disease. Besides, this was a person who had been committed to a hospital 20 years before under protest. He had vowed never to see a doctor again. No wonder he was so unrevealing to me.

I was very uneasy about the case. The diagnosis of intermittent alcoholism really did not say very much. Something was missing. When a therapist has this feeling, he or she should try to gather more information. Failing that, the therapist should wait until more information becomes available.

Mrs. Casey called two days before the next appointment and canceled it. She had a scheduling conflict, she told my secretary, and wanted to schedule another appointment for the following week. But she canceled again, saying that she and her husband were going on a 2-week vacation to California. She said she would call me when they returned.

I heard from her 3 weeks later. All was well. She and her husband were taking care of an old friend, a 79-year-old woman who was dying. Otherwise there were no problems. In fact, her husband had surprised her. After our second interview he had called his bank and had arranged to have 400 dollars transferred automatically from his account to hers every month.

That sort of thing is not uncommon in the course of therapy. A person will take action on something that has come up during the meetings without giving any indication that he or she has planned to do so. In fact, a person will sometimes take action even after he or she has rejected suggestions or advice to do so in the meeting. Mrs. Casey was so encouraged by the change in her husband that she saw no need for another appointment immediately. She said she'd call in 2 weeks just to keep in touch.

This time when she called there was urgency in her voice. The elderly friend had died 6 days before. For the past 4 days, her husband had been acting strange. She thought he was depressed. He seemed to be mentally absent at times when he was working in the yard. He would bend over, stare for 5 seconds and then freeze for several minutes. He looked pre-occupied and sometimes would not answer when she addressed him. He had begun saying *The Lord's Prayer* regularly before meals, had stood up once during a meal to pray, and just the day before had burned all of his past issues of *Playboy* magazine in the downstairs fireplace. His wife thought he had probably felt guilty reading them, but she was also worried that he might be getting ready to die. She was afraid. I offered them an appointment that afternoon.

She came alone; her husband had refused to come with her. He told her he was afraid of being "locked up." She believed he was struggling mightily for control and was dangerous. She decided to leave him again because she was afraid for her life.

I was worried too, but I had also begun to wonder about Mrs. Casey. Could it be that she was overreacting? She was fearful that her husband might kill himself or kill her but there was precious little evidence — save the incident 3 months ago – of his intentions to do either. What in fact was the situation, I wondered? And now Mr. Casey was no longer available to talk to. What should I do?

In search of more information, I asked Mrs. Casey's permission to call one of the daughters who lived in town and who had talked to her father recently. I phoned the daughter immediately and said, after introducing myself, "You probably know I've seen your parents a couple of times in the past six weeks. Something seems to be going wrong now and I'm not sure what it is. Your mother thinks your father is behaving strangely and she's worried. Do you have any observations or thoughts about all this that would help me out?"

She did indeed. She said that her mother had always been overemotional and controlling. She said I should give little credence to anything her mother said about her father. She hated to sound unsympathetic, she assured me, but wanted me to know that her mother was a difficult, manipulative person who had always been able to cry on a moment's notice to gain sympathy from people. The daughter also told me she had talked to her father on the telephone just 5 minutes before. He had seemed perfectly normal. In fact, she had invited her parents over for dinner that evening. Her father was also coming over in the afternoon to help her husband with some chores around the house.

I was now more confused than ever. This additional information from the Caseys' daughter made the situation even less understandable to me. I now possessed two wildly discrepant opinions about the same person. Now what?

I decided to again search for more information. I asked the daughter if she and her husband would be willing to join her parents and me within the next day or so for a family conference. She replied, with some irritation, that she doubted there was any real problem in the first place, that a conference was not necessary, and that she and her husband did not want to get involved with her parents' problems under any circumstances. Rather than throwing up my hands in frustration, I controlled by own impatience and tried a different tack: "You mentioned that you'd be seeing your father this afternoon. Would you be willing to phone me later today, after you've had a chance to see him for a few hours, and let me know if there's anything different about him?" She agreed.

She phoned just before 5:00 and said, "There's something obviously wrong with him. I've never seen him like this before. He can't seem to make decisions, he doesn't seem to be listening when you talk to him, and he looks preoccupied. He needs help."

I proposed that the whole family come in that evening or the next day. The daughter said that she would talk to her parents and her husband and call me later.

No call came. But 2 days later, a nurse in the emergency room at the medical school called me at home. She said that the Caseys had just arrived and wanted to talk to me. I went immediately. A change had indeed taken place in Mr. Casey. His wife had insisted he come to the emergency room after he had become unaccountably agitated in church. Now he sat rigidly in his chair, volunteering no information, looking bewildered. He denied that anything was wrong, as usual, and said that he was not depressed. I recommended that Mr. Casey enter the hospital for observation – he refused. I now thought that Mr. Casey probably had a serious depression, and I offered to treat him with antidepressants on the condition that he call me every other day on the telephone – this too he refused.

I faced a tough decision at this point. Could I in good conscience let the man go home or should I sign a psychiatric holding order which meant that the patient would have to spend 3 days in hospital before a court hearing about his mental state could take place? Based largely on his present strange condition and on the event of 3 months before, when Mr. Casey had threatened to kill his wife, I signed the holding order.

When I told Mr. Casey what I had done, he ran out of the emergency room. I was aware that he was frightened, but I wondered how I could have handled the situation better. Perhaps I had now irreconcilably alienated him, making further treatment impossible. Maybe it would have been better to let him go home and hope that he would call back at a later time.

The police brought Mr. Casey back to the emergency room 3 hours later. He had agreed to get in their car and return to the hospital; but when they arrived, he had struck one of the police officers, an act which virtually insured his admission.

A neurologic examination was immediately performed, and mildly increased reflexes in his right leg were noted. He had trouble with recent memory and recall. His fund of information was diminished when compared with my examination of 5 weeks before, and he was unable to copy a diamond on a piece of paper. Were these findings just artifacts associated with his fright and apprehension about being in hospital or were they really indicative of an underlying disorder? Another neurologic examination later that day, after he had been admitted to the ward, was completely normal, but the possibility that he had suffered a small stroke was still entertained.

He continued to be agitated for a day after his admission. He walked around restlessly, slept fitfully, and continually tried to negotiate with the staff for his release. He was edgy, irritable, and withdrawn. On the second evening in hospital, the resident in charge decided to order a medication, haloperidol, in an attempt to diminish his restlessness. It worked like a charm; by the next morning he had changed dramatically. He no longer paced aimlessly up and down the hall. He began to talk to the staff and to the other patients. He was seen to smile and he became cooperative with the staff. At his hearing, a day later, a judge decided that Mr. Casey was not a danger to himself or others. He was told that he could leave the hospital when he wished. But at the urging of the therapist, his wife, and the staff, he agreed to remain in hospital for another week while a complete workup could be carried out. An extremely thorough neurologic examination, which included a spinal tap, an electroencephalograph, and a brain scan, was done, all of which were normal. The earlier finding of increased reflexes in his right leg could never be replicated. His mental status examination was also normal on repeated testing. The resident psychiatrist on the ward, who also took a thorough history, concluded that Mr. Casey's drinking episodes were not associated with depression. He was discharged from the hospital without a diagnosis save periodic drinking.

I wondered if Mr. Casey had suffered from a small stroke which had cleared up spontaneously, as they often do. I also wondered if the death of the patient's older friend, interacting with a subtle dementing process, had caused an acute confusional episode. But the evidence was pretty thin. Everyone who had seen Mr. Casey was still unsatisfied, and still grasping for a diagnosis.

In the first outpatient visit after hospitalization, I told the Caseys that I was still uncertain about what had happened but that both of them should be prepared if another episode occurred. I asked Mrs. Casey to call me if she noticed anything wrong. I told Mr. Casey that a brief hospitalization might again be necessary in the future. He was by now much more friendly and spontaneous than I had ever seen him, and he agreed. We then proceeded to discuss some of the problems that the Caseys had had for a long time, independent of these crises, and we met several times to talk about the problems.

This was not the end of the story, however. After we had stopped meeting regularly, Mrs. Casey would phone every so often to tell me that things were calm. Her husband still did not talk much, but then he never had. The coupled planned to take a 3-week trip across the country in the middle of spring.

At the end of April, everything erupted again. Mrs. Casey phoned, desperately, to say that she thought her husband was drinking again. He looked preoccupied once more. He would stand up suddenly in the middle of dinner and stare straight ahead. While working in his yard, he would stop, hold himself in one position for a couple of minutes, not answer if addressed, then resume his work. She said that she could not stand it any more, and was determined to leave for good.

I asked them to come to my office immediately. I was struck by the change in Mr. Casey since I had seen him last. He said there was nothing wrong with him, of course, but he behaved so strangely. He looked around continually as if searching for a way out of the office. He occasionally stopped talking in midsentence and did not continue. He seemed distracted. He could not sit still and was clearly agitated. Twice during the interview he stood up and walked down the hall outside my office, as if he was in a daze, and returned only at my urging. Yet he was as clear as a bell on the mental status examination and another neurologic examination was normal. Contrary to his previous agreement with me, he refused to return to the hospital. Then he left abruptly.

Several hours later the daughter called. I was glad to hear from her. "Your father's in trouble again," I said, "I saw him earlier this afternoon. He's behaving quite strangely."

Daughter: My husband's worried about him too.
Therapist: Why?
Daughter: Well, he doesn't know much about it, but my father told him yesterday he hears God's voice.

Yes, of course; suddenly it all came together. Mr. Casey was hallucinating. This was the piece of information I needed to make the diagnosis. He was suffering from a paranoid disorder. It all added up: his distrust and suspiciousness of his wife — did this represent a long-standing delusion that she was unfaithful? — which lay behind his persistent refusal to give her money; his premorbid personality, characterized by solitariness, uncommunicativeness, and emotional aloofness; his normal mental status and neurologic examinations, which ruled out medical problems and an organic brain syndrome; his lack of depressive symptoms and my observation that he did not look depressed; his flat and unspontaneous countenance; his positive response to haloperidol; his preoccupied look, his blocking, his restlessness, his standing up in the middle of meals — he was probably hearing voices at those times.

Mr. Casey had no intention of returning to see me, however. I told his wife and daughter that Mr. Casey urgently needed help. The daughter refused to initiate commitment proceedings with her mother, feeling that her father needed an ally and that taking her mother's side now would permanently alienate her from her father. Mrs. Casey who had by this time left her husband, again asked me in desperation if I would be willing to be a signatory on a petition of mental illness. I said I would.

In the time it took to schedule and arrange a hearing, however, the patient unintentionally brought about his own remedy. When his wife left, he took it into his head that here was finally proof that his wife intended to run off with another man and make away with all his money. He imagined that an old Army friend of both of theirs, whom neither had seen in over 15 years, was her lover. He began to harass the man at his small clothing shop – he came into the store 16 times in three days – and finally hit the shopkeeper, who immediately called the police. Mr. Casey was brought swiftly to the hospital and a hold was signed. Three days later a judge committed him to the state hospital for 6 months, where he received proper treatment, the major part of which was antipsychotic medication. I talked with his wife several times after that. We discussed what had happened, her feelings about it, and what she could do to put his life together again. Six months later, Mr. Casey was discharged from the hospital, no longer delusional. He agreed to stay on medication. His wife accepted him back.

There are several points about this case that deserve emphasis. First, a knowledge of descriptive psychiatry is imperative in order to assess a patient properly. A therapist is called upon to help a wide variety of people, and he or she should not assume that all of them suffer from situational difficulties, neurotic disorders, or personality problems. Some are suffering from a serious mental disorder for which psychotherapy alone is useless. The therapist must be able to identify the nature of the problem that confronts him.

Second, the diagnosis of a paranoid illness could have been made sooner if more attention had been paid to some of the details in the patient's history. Of course a diagnosis always looks easier in retrospect, but a higher index of suspicion on my part would have helped. It is hard to maintain an open mind in a perplexing situation, and my attention was focused too narrowly on the possibilities of depression or of an organic brain syndrome.

Third, I was able to continue seeking information in the face of a very confusing situation. I kept the channels of communication open between myself and the patient's daughter, even when she was at first unhelpful. Instead of writing her off, however, I was able to contain my initial frus-

tration and stay in touch with her. The information she provided was ulti-
mately instrumental in resolving the case.

Appendix: A Psychiatric Write-Up

The following write-up was dictated after the first interview with a 26-year-old woman.

Date:	September 11, 1979
Name:	Katherine Abel
Address:	7815 S.W. Broadway, Portland, Oregon 97201
Phone numbers:	243–5698 (home), 280–4466 (work)
Insurance:	Blue Cross of Oregon
Birthdate:	August 3, 1953

Katherine Abel is a 26-year-old single white woman who was referred to me by Dr. John Lewis in internal medicine. He told me Miss Abel had a long history of nausea and vomiting which became so severe that last week she came to the emergency room because she was severely dehydrated. He told me also that she was an intelligent, undisclosing person who was reluctant to admit that she had any personal problems. I said I would be glad to see her.

Miss Abel's major complaint is intermittent episodes of nausea and vomiting for the last 13 years. The first episode occurred when she was 13, in the 7th grade. She was attending a private school. On the day school began, she found out that her classes would not be held in the building she had been told they would. She was also told that she would have to move from room to room for each class during the day rather than remain in just one room for all her classes, as she had been used to doing in earlier grades. This information upset her. She decided not to return to school the next day, telling her parents she felt sick. After 2 days at home, however, her parents insisted she return to school and escorted her there forcibly. She vomited on the doorstep of the school as she was entering the building.

She has been troubled by nausea and vomiting ever since. There have been three such episodes in the last 3 months, each of which has lasted 3 to 6 days. The first episode occurred immediately after she asked her boy friend to live with her. She was apprehensive and uncertain about her decision, and was unsure about whether he would accept her invitation or not. She vomited about nine times in 3 days. A month later (they were now living together), he decided to visit a friend in California and did not tell her when he would return. He came back 5 days after he left. She began vomiting on the day he returned. She was furious with him for not telling her how long he would be gone but was unable to express her feelings directly. She has always had trouble expressing her feelings directly to people.

The most serious episode of vomiting began 8 days ago. Her boy friend unexpectedly announced that he wanted to visit friends in Washington state. He wanted her to come and meet several of his old friends. His decision was entirely too sudden for her; she wanted more time to plan. Besides, she has always had trouble meeting new people and dealing with new situations. But she went with him anyway, without telling him of her anxiety and irritation. The day after they arrived she began vomiting. She continued to vomit for 6 days, five to six times a day, until she became so weak and discouraged that she came to the hospital for help. She was given several liters of fluid in the course of one afternoon and evening, then discharged. She has not vomited for the past two days.

There is one other situation in which she inevitably vomits: when she visits her parents in California. She feels controlled by them. She has never been able to talk freely or easily about her feelings with either of them. She writes them infrequently, though she receives a letter once a week from her mother.

I learned only a little about her past history: she was born and raised in Oakland, California; her father is an accountant, her mother a homemaker; she has a sister 6 years younger than herself; her parents were always strict and demanding. Miss Abel felt loved but not always accepted for who she was; her parents to this day press her to make a professional career of some kind. The family members all kept their feelings hidden. In recent years, Miss Abel's mother has been drinking heavily, and the patient believes her mother is depressed. Her mother sometimes stays in bed with vague abdominal complaints. There is no history of mental illness in the family.

At the moment, she works as a laboratory technician for a professor of chemistry at Portland State University. His grant – and her job – runs out in another 8 months. She is uncertain about the future after her job ends.

She describes herself as a compulsive person: she keeps lists; she likes things in order; she makes detailed plans. She showed me a health chart that she has kept since the beginning of the year. It was neat, readable, and comprehensive.

She has a number of assets. She has worked regularly for the last 3 years and enjoys her job. She gets along reasonably well with co-workers. She has a small circle of good friends whom she sees regularly. She has one close woman friend. She plays the piano well and enjoys hiking. Her physical health has been good. She has never consulted a psychiatrist before. In times of stress, she seems to use the coping mechanisms of suppression, somatization, and intellectualization. I estimate that her intelligence is well above average.

In our meeting today, Miss Abel is dressed in jeans, a light print shirt, and hiking boots. She is tall, about 5 feet, 7 inches, and has a lanky build and a thin face with sharp features. Her hair is dark brown and slightly curly; her eyes are also brown. She is tense during most of the interview. She has a precise, formal way of speaking; she also tends to talk in generalities but is easily able to provide me with specific examples when I ask for them. She does not look depressed and shows a normal range of affect. Her vocabulary is very good, her memory excellent.

She impresses me as a shy, intellectual, somewhat compulsive person. She says she would like to gain control of her nausea and vomiting episodes. I think we can work together. The problem list is as follows·

1. Episodes of nausea and vomiting in situations where she feels unable to express her underlying feelings.
2. Underassertiveness with some people, e.g., boy friend and parents.

Formulation: Miss Abel has episodes of nausea and vomiting when she has strong feelings that she cannot or will not express directly. This pattern was established early in her life. Feelings – anxiety or anger – toward her boy friend have precipitated the most recent episodes. She is, in general, a shy, inhibited person who values orderliness and regularity; unexpected events seem to upset her easily. Her current symptoms distress her not only because she feels she has no control over them, but also because she becomes weak and, as in the last episode, very ill. What I know about her family leads me to suspect that her parents, whom she views as demanding, emotionally unexpressive, and orderly themselves, played a large role in shaping their daughter's personality in the direction of shyness, orderliness, and emotional unexpressiveness. By discouraging or perhaps by ignoring verbal expressions of feelings on the part of their children, they forced Miss Abel to find another, more demonstrative way of expressing herself.

Miss Abel has a number of personality assets, as I mentioned earlier.

DIAGNOSIS

Axis I: Psychological factors affecting physical condition, contribution definite.
Axis II: Compulsive traits; no personality disorder.
Axis III: Intermittent emesis.
Axis IV: Psychosocial stress: Interpersonal conflict with boy friend. Severity 4 moderate.
Axis V: Highest level of adaptive functioning past year; 3 good.

PLAN

1. In the next few sessions, I would like to know more about Miss Abel's
    a. History after high school: education, relationships, etc.
    b. Current patterns of living and relating to other people, particularly her boy friend.
    c. Methods of coping with other stressful events.
    d. History of nausea and vomiting: other precipitating events, frequency of episodes.
2. I have asked Miss Abel to make a list of the kinds of situations that lead to episodes of nausea and vomiting between now and our next visit.
3. I suggested to her that her vomiting may be a way of expressing herself when she has strong feelings. If that's true — and she thinks it may be — encouraging her to be more direct in her expression of feelings may be helpful. We'll talk more about this next visit.
4. We meet again September 19, 1979, at 3:00.

Index

a
b
c
d
e
f
g
0 h
1 i
8 2 j